FACING JOB
Interviews

Published by
Lotus Press Publishers & Distributors

FACING JOB
Interviews

Marry Stella

4735/22, Prakash Deep Building
Ansari Road, Darya Ganj,
New Delhi-110002

Lotus Press Publishers & Distributors
Unit No.220, 2nd Floor, 4735/22, Prakash Deep Building,
Ansari Road, Daryaganj, New Delhi - 110002
Ph.: 32903912, 23280047, 09811838000
E-mail : lotus_press@sify.com
Visit us : www.lotuspress.co.in

Facing Job Interviews
© 2014, Marry Stella
ISBN: 81-89093-94-0

Published by : Lotus Press Publishers & Distributors, New Delhi-110002
Printed at : A.J. Book Binding House, Delhi

Contents

Preface

What is an interview? It is not life or death, the apocalypse, or a standardised text. An interview is a conversation about possibilities, a chance to learn, and an opportunity to share information. Make the most of your interview—relax, take the time to respond, and be yourself.

In a job interview, the employer tries to choose the best person for the job, and the candidate tries to prove that he is the suitable person for it.

A successful candidate needs to plan what he wants to say, prepare questions and practise answering them. He must establish his ability through his resume by placing emphasis on accomplishments and results from precious jobs. Good communication skill is essential in dealing with customers, clients or management, hence good interpersonal skills are essential.

Instead of focusing on what you want, focus on what the employer wants, and you will land that much coveted job!

1
Introduction

An interview is the most popular way to assess an individual to ascertain if he or she is suitable for a role within a company. The interview is normally the second step to successfully obtaining employment with a company, following the submittance of an application-form with an enclosed curriculum vitae.

The interview is an opportunity for an employer to get to know the candidate behind the resume. It is also a chance for candidates to get a sense of a company culture, values and plans for the future.

How do you face an interview? This is a crucial issue for many young job seekers. It is a stage where they need to be wary, as they may possibly be entering a vocation. (1) What is a CV? (2) How do you dress? (3) How do you respond to tricky questions? and (4) English Communication are some of the areas that may pose problems for the aspiring job seeker.

Job interviews are perhaps the most important part of the selection process, for both the job seeker and the future employer. Once the candidate's resume (or/and a written initial test) has been taken and some candidates have been shortlisted amongst the lot, that is, it has been established that the candidate

1

meets the basic skills and background requirements, it is the interview that establishes him/her as a candidate who will fit well into an organisation's culture and future plans.

The best job interviews are respectful encounters that allow mutual discovery. It may feel as if the employer has all the power. After all, it is the employer who will decide whether to offer you the job. Ultimately, however, it is you who hold the power, because it will be you who decides whether to accept the job or not. So, interviews are just as important for you in the selection process as they are for the interviewer. Keep that power balance in mind, and it will help you stay calm, dignified, and have a clear thinking when tricky questions are asked.

Job interviews are critical to the quality of an organisation's people. Good job interviews, processes and methods increase the quality of people in an organisation. Poor job interview methods result in poor selection, which undermines organisational capabilities, wastes management time, and increases staff turnover.

Interviews are always stressful, even for job seekers who have gone on countless interviews. Interviews are all about making the best matches. Both the company and the job seeker want to determine if there is a correct fit between them.

The interview can be the most daunting aspect of searching for work, but can also have the most impact on your salary and benefits package if you are successful in obtaining employment.

An interview assesses your suitability for the position that you are applying for. There are several types of interviews, and the company may elect to use more than one to select its employers. Some are more formal than others, and it is wise to establish the type of interview you will be attending so that you can be fully prepared.

Effective job interviewing is the key to getting the job you want. A job interview is similar in many ways to a social conversation, but is requires more than just conversational skills. How well you do in a job interview will depend on how will you can elaborate on your accomplishments and qualifications, as they relate to what the employer wants and needs.

Interviews are particularly useful for getting the story behind a participant's experiences. The interviewer can pursue in depth information around a topic. Interviews may be useful as follow-up to certain respondents to questionnaires, e.g., to further investigate their responses.

An interview levels the playing field, no matter where you went to school or college, no matter what your grades are, no matter how much experience you have, no matter who you know — if you are not able to interview successfully, you won't get the job.

An interview has a specific purpose. It generally follows a fairly set pattern, time, place, duration, participants and subject matter. These are prepared well in advance. The interview is conducted by one group or two people (or by a single person) who manage the proceedings. Generally, the interviewer asks the questions initially, while the candidate contributes the answers, and may then finally ask questions of the interviewer.

By its nature the interview creates a tense and often daunting atmosphere between people. The interviewer and the interviewee have different roles to play, and are not equal partners. In such an unnatural or artificial setting, it would be foolish to expect to feel at ease, both for the interviewer as well as the candidate. But with good preparation, and a calm attitude, adopting various strategies, you should be able to cope or even shine in the interview room.

When interviews are held in the workplace, bosses or personnel managers conduct interviews. The interview may be to select new staff; it may be for a promotion; it may be an appraisal interview; or to deal with disciplinary problems.

It is very clear that there is inequality between the participants.— the interviewer and the interviewee. While the former has the power to employ, upgrade or fire the interviewee, the interviewee has to prove his mettle to be the first choice among a horde of other participants. If he fails to make a mark at the interview he will be the loser, but if the interviewer chooses the wrong candidate for the job, the company as a whole suffers. So an interview is an important arena for the participants to course their future.

PART - I
The Interviewer

2
Preparing an Interview

The interviewer is the person seated directly across from the candidate, and charged with leading the conversation. Sometimes this person is a professional especially trained to assess candidates fit for the job. More often, however, he or she is doing this work in conjunction with a larger job description. In this case, the interviewer could be burdened with a difficult attitude about the meeting; for example, being resentful at have to be yanked away from his regular duties, or being shy or confused about what kinds of results to expect from the interview.

The responsibilities of the interviewer are not merely confined to making the right selection. Within the interview room he has to exercise courtesy and show consideration towards the candidates.

Being the host, the interviewer should observe the normal formalities of social interchange. Not only is this common decency but is also aimed at maintaining the company's reputation.

Most candidates may be first-time interviewees, and the interview gives them a first peep into the workings of the company or group. The heightened atmosphere of the interview may have a lasting impression on the candidates, and such an impression is largely created by the interviewer.

Treat all the applicants fairly. Even if they are rejected for various reasons, at least they will carry away good impressions of the company. Antagonise them, and they will always criticise the company whenever they have an opportunity to do so. If these antagonised candidates do get into some top positions elsewhere, their poor impression of your company could lead to lost business for your company.

Your first task as an interviewer would start with the preparation of the advertisement for the position. Make sure you get out your advertisement in time. Too many people leave advertising until the last moment, and have to rush the whole hiring process. By adopting a consistent format for advertisements, you can save yourself a lot of trouble.

The advertisement should include the following:

a) your company logo.

b) your company name.

c) a brief description of the duties.

d) a brief description of the kind of applicant you are looking for, with details of experience demanded, and qualifications.

e) a direct statement of the pay offered.

f) a clear statement of what kind of reply is required, to whom, where, and before when.

g) say whether references are requested at this stage.

Consider the skills, qualifications and personal qualities you are looking for. Don't forget to look beyond the most obvious requirements. For example, consider the importance of a candidates ability to work in a team or in isolation, to lead or to follow, to be creative or to reproduce accurately someone else's pattern of work.

If you are able to be very specific in your requirements, there will be fewer number of unsuitable candidates applying.

Use of Job Applications and Resumes

Get the most of these pre-screening tools by understanding what to look for. Two important tools in pre-screening are the resume and the employment application. If you ask applicants to send in a resume, that will be the first tool you use to screen them. You have qualified candidates fill out an application when they come in for an interview. If you don't ask for a resume, you will probably want to have prospective employees come in and fill out applications, then review the applications and call qualified candidates to set up an interview.

In either case, it is important to have an application form ready before you begin the interview process. You can develop your own application form to meet your specific needs.

The job application form presents a further opportunity for narrowing down the list of applications, and selecting a short-list for interview. To be effective, the wording in any application form is very important; think carefully about the question it poses.

Your application form should ask for specific information such as name, address and phone number; educational background; work experience, including salary levels; awards or honours; whether the applicant can work full or part time as well as available hours; and any special skills relevant to the job (foreign languages, familiarity with software programmes, etc.). Be sure to ask for names and phone numbers of former supervisors to check as references; if the candidate is currently employed, ask whether it is all right to contact his or her current place of employment. You may also want to ask for personal references.

Job application forms make sifting easy. Those forms which immediately reveal that a candidate is underqualified or semiliterate, or a fresher with absolutely no experience whatsoever can be outrightly rejected without wasting time. But remember to send out courtesy letters of rejection to them.

You will face problems when you have to decide about borderline candidates. By wording the questions cleverly in the job application form, you will be spared the trouble of deciding which of these applicants you really feel are worth interviewing . It will also help provide useful information for the interview.

The information for the interview can be background and foreground information. Background information includes work experience, relevant skills, such as a knowledge of foreign languages, and so on.

Foreground information includes typically the candidate's attitudes, outside interests, or even irrelevant skills, for example, a question about his driving licence.

Since many employees these days hesitate to give out information about an employee, you may want to have the applicant sign a waiver that states the employee authorises former and/or current employers to disclose information about him or her.

Screening Resumes

When you start screening resumes, it helps to have your job description and other particulars in front of you so that the qualities and skills that you are looking for are clearly etched in your mind.

Evaluating resumes can be very subjective since there is no set standard or form for resumes. However, certain specifics may be expected in a resume. It should contain the prospect's name, address and telephone number at the top, and a brief summary of employment and educational background, including dates. Many resumes include a 'career objective' that describes what kind of job the prospect is pursuing. Other applicants state their objectives in their cover letters. Any additional information you may find furnished in a resume or in covering letter includes references, achievements and career-related affiliations.

What you need to look for in the applicant's resume and covering letter are neatness and professionalism. A resume that is riddled with too many corrections, or grammatical or spelling errors raises some serious doubts. If the candidate is unable to take care during this crucial stage of his career, how can you expect him to fare well in his job if he is employed?

There are two basic types of resumes. The chronological resume and the functional resume. The former type is the one that we generally get to see. It lists employment history in reverse chronological order from the most recent position to the first. The functional resume does not list dates of employment, but it lists skills or functions that the employee has performed.

In recent years, the trend shows the popularity of functional resumes. In some cases, they are used by downsized executives who may be quite well qualified, and are simply trying to downplay long periods of employment. In other cases, however, they signal that the applicant is a job hopper or has something to hide.

Many people are prone to embellish their resumes. Therefore, it is better to have the candidates fill out a job application by mail or in person and then compare with their resume. Since your application requires information to be completed in a chronological order, it gives you a more accurate picture of an applicant's real history.

There is something more important that outweighs the functional and chronological resumes. It is the responsibility resume, as opposed to the accomplishment resume, which emphasises the job description. For example,"I managed three account executives, established budgets, developed new techniques in sales," etc. An accomplishment resume, on the other hand, emphasises accomplishments and results, such as, "I cut costs by 50 per cent; met quota every month," etc. Such a resume tells you that the candidate is an achiever, and has the bottom line firmly in place.

While reading the resume, try to determine the candidate's career patterns, look for steady progress and promotions in past jobs. Also, look for stability in terms of length of employment. If a person is a rolling stone, changing jobs frequently, he is probably not someone you want on your team. Look for people who have put in five to six-year job stints.

You must also consider how economic conditions can affect a person's resume. During a climate of frequent corporate downsizing, for example, a series of lateral career moves may signal that a person is a survivor. This also shows that the person is interested in growing and willing to take on new responsibilities, even if there was no corresponding increase in pay or status. By the same token, first because a resume or a job application has a few gaps in it does not mean that you should overlook it entirely. Stay focused on the skills or value the job applicant could bring to your company.

Starting with Job Description

Your advertisement shows a vacant position in your company, and a stack of applications pour in by the time limit as stated in the advertisement. Most of them may seem to meet or exceed the minimum qualifications for the job. Now it is time to begin narrowing the pool down to a handful of finalist candidates whom you wish to interview. How do you approach the project?

You should have already worked out how to develop a comprehensive and uptodate job description. Use that description as the basis for your thinking. You are looking for candidates who show clear evidence that they have performed comparable work, and have the skills and background to do the job for which you are hiring.

A good job description defines what you consider to be the essential criteria for doing the job — and for doing it well. You should use these criteria to objectively evaluate each candidate's qualifications.

Developing a Chart

Consider developing a criterion chart before you look at the applications. List the names of the candidates across the top. Then list down the side the following criteria, taken directly from the job description:

a) The education requirements

b) The years-of-experience requirements

c) The five or ten most important job duties or responsibilities of the position

d) The five or ten most critical interpersonal or interactive skills required of the position.

Ranking the Candidates

You can rank each candidate in the resulting grid on a scale of 0-10, based on the evidence that they present which indicates that they have the required skill, or have performed duties comparable to those you are looking for.

Advantages of Grids

Making a grid has a number of useful advantages.

1. It creates an automatic first set of notes that you can refer back to during your interviewing process.

2. It allows you to concentrate on one applicant at a time, instead of trying to juggle and compare everyone at once in your head.

3. If an unsuccessful candidate files a discrimination complaint against you for failure to hire, it creates a handy

document that can help establish the fact that you used legitimate, job-related criteria in making your decisions.

Consider the following suggestions before filling in the grid or chart:

1. At the outset, look at all the applications, ignoring the names. Check the overall skills and qualifications available to you in the applicant pool. This will help you to estimate an average level among the candidates' skills and experience. The average that you see will become a 5 in your mind. Doing this will help you avoid giving the first candidate you see a 10 (or a 1), and then picking up the second application and wanting to give an even higher (or lower) score. After you have got a sense of the average, shuffle the applications, and review and score them individually in random order.

2. Allot points only when there is concrete or direct evidence that a skill, knowledge or experience exists. Avoid stretching to make inferences of a skill that may or may not be there. It is the applicant's responsibility to furnish you with full details and if he has not done so, do not guess or assume. If there is no evidence one way or another on a certain skill or experience, give no points, or write NE (no evidence) in the grid. When the whole grid has been filled in, total your points across the bottom of the grid.

Watch for Discrepancies

Have sheets of paper handy, while you review, one sheet for each applicant. As you proceed with the review, make notes of questions that crop up in your mind. Watch out for any sort of discrepancies, like unexplained gaps in employment history or inconsistent information. Be careful not to miss vague dates and be cautious of minimal or questionable descriptions of responsibilities.

If the position requires good written or verbal communication skills, for example, look out for carelessness such as typing errors, poor grammar, or lack of clarity. These are issues that you would want to tackle with the candidate if you decide to interview him. Attach your notes to each set of application materials for later reference.

Some details of background information may startle you if disclosed only in the interview-that the applicant is handicapped in some way, for instance, or that he is the chairman's nephew. To avoid being taken unawares, try to include a catch-all question on the application form, like:

"Mention any other personal or professional details that you feel may have some bearing on your application."

Foreground information may have topics for exploration in the interview-typically, the candidate's attitudes, outside interests, or 'irrelevant' skills. For example, a question about the applicants driving licence—this might provide a lead into discussing relocation or multi-site work.

Once you have narrowed down your pool to three or four strong candidates, schedule interviews. But before you bring in your first applicant, some preliminary planning will help you ensure a successful interview process.

Preparing Interview Questions in Advance

Job interviews are stressful situations, both for the candidate and the interviewer. Interviewing is not something that most hiring managers do often enough to develop great comfort with.

You must realise that good interview questions seldom crop up into your head during an interview. You can't really listen to a candidate's answer to one question if you are trying to think up the next question at the same time. So it is always a good idea to evolve in advance a written set of core questions that you will ask every candidate.

By asking all candidates the same basic set of questions, you accomplish several things:

a) You give each candidate an equal opportunity to speak about the things you are interested in.

b) You receive comparable information on all candidates, so that it is easier to rate them.

c) You reduce your legal risk if your hiring decision is challenged by a candidate alleging differential treatment during an interview.

Criterion-based Questions

The questions you write should be derived directly from the criteria you articulated in the job description. The questions should evoke from the candidate revealing information about the technical skills they have, about how they handle interactions with others they come into contact with, and about the work they have done before, and how it compares with your needs. You should prepare at least 10 or more good questions that will help you evaluate how the person would do in the job you have.

If you are interviewing for an administrative assistant for your academic department, for example, you can ask criterion-based questions like these:

"This position requires that you keep tract of ordering departmental supplies and equipment, and make sure we stay within the budget. Describe for me a time when you have had to do something similar in other jobs."

"This position is one that supports the work of eight busy faculty members, all of whom want their project done yesterday-and ahead of everyone else's. Have you ever had a job where you have had to handle many busy professionals with competing priorities? If so, what were your strategies for "Juggling the work and maintaining successful working relationships?"

Behaviour-based Questions

Apart from designing questions that reflect the essential functions of the job, design the questions in a way that will elicit genuine, thoughtful, and detailed responses rather than 'canned' answers. Avoid questions that elicit only 'yes' or 'no' answers.

Behaviour-based questions require the individual to tell you stories about how they have handled specific situations in the past-situations that are comparable to those they will face in your position. For example, for a position requiring strong customer-service skills, you might require candidates to "describe a specific incident when you were confronted by an irate customer, and tell me specifically how you handled the situation."

Avoid hypothetical questions. Don't ask, "How would you handle so and so?" but rather, "How have you handled so and so?" You don't want them to give you speculative answers about how they might handle a situation in a perfect case. Rather, you want to know how they have handled such situations. Remember the best predictor of future behaviour is past behaviour. And the best way to get at past behaviour is to phrase your questions along these lines:

"This job will require xxx. Talk to me about a time when you have done xxx, and describe for me how you did it successfully."

"How did you tackle the problem like xxx in your previous job? Give me some specific examples."

"Describe the experience you have had doing xxx."

"What are the sorts of job that you handle well on your own, and what things do you find more comfortable with structured supervision?"

"In this job you are expected to handle xxx types of people in xxx sorts of situations. Compare these to what you have done before."

"What would your current loss describe as your real strengths, and what would be likely described as areas where you would benefit from constructive coaching or mentoring?"

"There is something about your work experience that I wondered about as I went through your application. Can you help me understand it?"

Telephone or In-person Interviews

Once you have formulated your core interview questions, consider whether you want to conduct telephone interviews before inviting people to your office. The advantages lie in situations where:

a) You may be flooded with applicants who look qualified on paper, and you want to narrow down the pool to a few top candidates.

b) You have the candidates who otherwise would have to come in from out of town.

If you decide to interview some candidates by phone, then you should conduct only phone interviews, so that all those interviewed are treated equitably.

Set aside enough time to conduct interviews of substance. This will enable you to save time and money, as also for the candidate.

Telephone interviews should be scheduled in advance, just like in-person interviews, so the candidates have time to prepare. Of course, if face-to-face interactive skills are essential for the job, phone interviews may not be the best option, even as a preliminary screening process. Even if you do conduct preliminary phone interviews, you will almost certainly want to invite your finalists to visit in person.

For most positions, it is not always possible to conduct a comprehensive and carefully thought out interview, with behaviour-based questions and answers, in less than one to one and a half hours. Most professional positions, especially those that demand several years of experience, or those that involve search committees or interviews with multiple reviewers, will take considerably more time.

In addition to the immediate supervisor, try involving others in the interview process. For example, you can include peer co-workers, primary constituents or managers from other sections, who have interaction with the department involved. But make sure that they ask all candidates the same core questions, and that they have their notes.

The main advantage in involving others too is the wealth of perspective that multiple opinions can provide. Another advantage is that people who were able to provide feedback on the selection may have more vested interest in helping the new employee to succeed as a member of the team.

Since you want the candidates to really understand the job for which they are applying give each finalist a copy of the job description. This will allow both you and the candidates to assess whether their skills and experiences are a good match for your needs. It will be advantageous to you as well as them if you send them a copy of the job description in advance of the interview. This will enable them to consider their interview responses within the context of the job, and they can ask informed questions to clarify their own understanding.

It is important to communicate a timeframe for the interview. This allows the applicant to have a reasonable expectation of how long you need to conduct the interview. They will need to plan and schedule a realistic amount of time. Be sure that when you plan on, say, two hours, then stick to it.

Scheduling Candidates

A letter or a phone call is sufficient to arrange an interview with a candidate. Be prepared to provide the following information in your letter or phone call.

1) Directions to the venue where the interview is scheduled to take place.

2) The date, time and expected duration of the interview.

3) The interview format - whether it will one-to-one, with a group, etc.

4) Any materials they should bring with them to complete or supplement their application-portfolio of work examples, letter of recommendation, transcripts, etc.

5) An interview itinerary, when the candidate will be involved in several interview meetings.

Considerations for Out-of-town Candidates

When you invite a candidate for the interview from out of town, it is best to confirm all arrangements in writing. Some additional considerations are:

1) Travel costs for the candidates must be borne by your company. So plan accordingly.

2) If you are reimbursing their train fare, inform them accordingly. Be specific about whether the candidate is expected to travel by first or second class, or in an air-conditioned coach.

3) Be also specific about whether you plan to meet both their to and fro charges or whether it is just one-way journey.

4) You will also need to agree with the candidate about who will make any hotel reservations and pay the tab, arrange for transportation from the railway station (or airport, if travelling by air) to the interview site or hotel, and pay for meals.

5) You should provide an itinerary or agenda for the day's interviews, and make advance arrangements to get the candidate from one meeting to the next.

6) Finally, schedule a tour of the company.

Conclusion

In a nutshell Conclusion, the following points need to be borne in mind:

1) Choose a setting with little distraction. Avoid loud lights or noises, and ensure the interviewee is comfortable (you might ask them if they are), etc. Often, they may feel more comfortable with just one person interviewing, or in their own places of work or homes.

2) Arrange the seating in an informal relaxed way. Don't sit behind a desk directly facing the interviewee. Sit around a coffee table or meeting room table.

3) Clear your desk, apart from what you need for the interview, so it shows that you have prepared and are organised, which shows you respect the situation and the interviewee.

4) Before you start to design your interview questions and process, clearly articulate to yourself what problem or need is to be addressed, using the information to be gathered by the interviews. This helps you keep a clear focus on the intent of each question.

5) You must make notes of the questions you intend to ask, otherwise you will forget.

6) Decide on the essential things you need to learn and prepare questions to prove them.

7) Plan the environment–privacy, no interruptions, ensure the interviewee is looked after while they wait.

8) What employers or interviewers should look for in a job interview are qualifications, positive attitude, interest in the company and position, stable work history, clear sense of purpose, communication skills, and high performance standards.

3

Forms of Interview

All candidates are entitled to know beforehand what form the interview will take, how long it will last, how many interviewers will be present and so on. This is a courteous gesture that one extends to the candidates in advance.

The type of interview chosen by the employer is determined by a number of factors, including personal preference of the interviewer, the history and customs of the organisation, the cost, administrative/legal requirements, and the wish to use modern interviewing techniques perceived to be more effective, e.g., behaviour-based interviewing, panel interviews, group interviews, one-to-one interviews, structured and unstructured interviews, telephone interviews, etc.

Interviews are becoming increasingly popular as a research tool. Since the earliest day of psychology, the interview has been seen as a useful way of collecting data, but the method was not seen as 'scientific' by the behaviourist school, although even behaviourists acknowledged that what they called 'verbal behaviour' sometimes provides useful research data.

An interview occurs when a participant is asked questions that have been designed to elicit particular types of information. Interviewing is a skilled activity, because of its inter-personal nature. People are very good at reading non-verbal signs, i.e., the small changes in behaviour that indicate how information is being received. These are often unconscious on the part of the interviewer, but they can have a profound effect on the way people respond.

In a face-to-face situation, for example, most people like to be cooperative, and to avoid interpersonal conflict. So an unconscious indication from an interviewer that they disagree with what the person has said, or with a particular option in a question, can lead respondents to change their answers to something that they feel is more socially acceptable.

Any social situation also means that people will bring their wider social knowledge and habits into the situation, and this can affect the answers they give. It is not uncommon that people respond differently to male interviewers than they do to female interviewers. Age and ethnicity may also have an effect.

Basically, people adjust their responses according to what they consider appropriate for the person asking the questions.

Interviewer effects of this kind are something which need to be taken into account in any interview study. If the study is concerned with obtaining representative views from a large number of people, then it is more likely that more than one interviewer is needed, and then it is appropriate to counterbalance interviewer effects by varying age, gender and ethnicity so that it is balanced out in the sample as a whole.

The interviewer asks the questions, and the interviewee (respondent) answers the questions. Interviews may be formal, directive interviews and more informal interviews.

There are many number of interview situations you can find yourself in beyond the 'normal' routine of one interviewer, one interviewer's desk and little old you. Nowadays, you need to be prepared for the 'screening' interview, the 'committee' interview, the 'lunch' interview, etc.

The interviews can be traditional or behaviour based.

Traditional (or Structured) Interviews

Traditional questions are direct, and tend to give the interviewee the sense that he is being tested, as if there are right and wrong answers.

Traditional questions might be something like these:
1) Why do you want to work for this campany?
2) Why do you want to hold this position?
3) Aside from money, what will you gain from having this job?
4) Tell me your strengths and weaknesses.

Interviewing success or failure are more often based on the ability of the job-seeker to communicate than on the truthfulness or content of their answers. Employers are looking for the answer to three questions:
1) Does the job-seeker have the skills and abilities to perform the job?
2) Does the job-seeker possess the enthusiasm and work ethic that the employer expects?
3) Will the job-seeker be a team player, and fit into the organisation?

The strength of the structured or guided interview is that it keeps interaction focused, covering the same ground with respondent sets, while allowing individual experience to emerge. The weakness lies in that it cannot divert far, or long, from the agenda, without losing part of 'the story'.

In a structured interview, the questions have to answered in a pre-set order, strict schedule, same questions and same order.

The answers can be quantified, or put into numbers, and statistical analysis can be performed.

The advantage is that fixed questions are easier for the interviewer to conduct (especially to conduct survey with large samples). The responses are more objectively verifiable and generalisable.

The disadvantages are the problem with the interview approach and validity. There is lack of reliability.

When different interviewers use the same structure questioned this can be a disadvantage. The interviewers must be trained in the same way because they need to use the same techniques in order to have a consistent approach to the respondents. When interviewers depart from the interview schedule, they may elicit information that biases further answers.

Inter-interviewer reliability is obtained if the same training has been given to the interviewers, and that they all follow the interview schedule in structured interviews. It may also help to make pilot studies to train the interviewers.

In the structured interview, all important points are explored during the interview and helps guarantee that all applicants are treated fairly and equitably.

Behaviour-based Interview

Behavioural interviewing is the process by which interviewers gather and evaluate information about a potential employee's past performance to judge how he or she would respond in future situations. By asking job-seekers to answer hypothetical questions interviewers hope to get an accurate indication of how candidates will perform as employees.

More and more employers are conducting a different type of interview than they did five or ten years ago. These interviews are filled with behaviour-based questions designed to elicit patterns of accomplishments relevant to the employer's situation. They are specific and challenge interviewees to provide concrete examples of their achievements in different types of situations. Such interviews are based on the simple belief that how a job candidate has responded to certain types of situations in the past is a good predictor of how that person will behave in a similar future situation.

The premise behind behavioural interviewing is that the most accurate predictor of future performance is past performance in similar situations. Behavioural interviewing, in fact, is said to be 55 per cent predictor of future on-the-job behaviour, while traditional interviewing is only 10 per cent predictive.

Behaviour-based interview is the most popular form of interviewing used by many recruiters. In order to put together a list of the selection criteria for various positions, most employers will look at the top performers within their organisation, and identify which skills knowledge and/or personal qualities they have which make them effective in their positions. In the interview, their aim will be to gain evidence that the applicant possesses the particular combination of selection criteria that they are looking for. They will do this by asking the candidate to give specific examples of what they have done that would demonstrate that they possess the particular selection criteria required for that position. The questions are usually quite detailed, and the question will often be fairly consistent.

Behaviour-based interviews use past behaviour as a predictor of future performance. This interview method is also referred to as 'targeted selection'. Applicants have to be able to give specific examples of their experiences as a way of showing that they can meet the critical requirements of a job. In theory, such interviews should involve a number of interviewers, though this is not always the case. Behaviour-based interviews can be understood by contrasting a couple of common interview questions. In each example, the question is presented (a) in a straight or direct format, and then (b) as a behavioural question.

Example 1

a) Are you good at problem solving?

b) Describe a problem you have been asked to solve. What did you do? What alternative did you consider? Did you succeed or fail? Why?

Example 2

a) How do you go about making decisions?

b) Give me an example of a good decision you have made recently. What were the alternatives you considered? Why was it a good decision?

Behavioural simulations, creating a work-related scenario, can be used to supplemental information collected during the interview. For example, in an interview for a position which requires a lot client contact and customer service, the following workplace problem could be presented: "Imagine your major client phones on a Saturday afternoon with a problem which requires immediate attention and a solution before Monday morning. However, you have committed yourself to a social weekend with your immediate supervisor and other managers who may be able to assist your progress through the organisation. What is your response to this situation?"

Your answers to such simulations can reveal your approach to prioritising problem solving, loyalty and commitment. In preparing for such interviews, you need to carefully research the qualities required to carry out the job, and then reflect on how your previous experiences could be relevant, and could be used to demonstrate your competence and suitability. Real experiences, not simply what you might do in hypothetical situations, give the interviewers an idea of your ability.

As stated earlier, the behavioural job interview is based on the theory that past performance is the best indicator of future behaviour, and uses questions that prove specific past behaviours, such as:

1) Tell me about a time where you confronted an unexpected problem.

2) Tell me about an experience when you failed to achieve a goal.

3) Give me a specific example of a time when you managed several projects at once.

Job-seekers need to prepare for these interviews by recalling scenarios that fit the various types of behavioural interviewing questions. Expect interviewers to have several follow-up questions and probe for details that explore all aspects of a given situation or experience.

Behavioural interviewing is a relatively new mode of job interviewing. Increasing numbers of employers are using behaviour-based methods to screen job candidates, and understanding how to excel in this interview environment is becoming a crucial job-hunting skill.

Behaviour-based interviewing is touted as providing a more objective set of facts to make employment decisions than other interviewing methods. Traditional interview questions are general, while the process of behavioural interviewing is much more probing, and works very differently.

In a traditional job interview, you can usually get away with telling the interviewer what he or she wants to hear, even if you are fudging a bit on the truth. Even if you are asked situational questions that start out with "How would you handle xxx situation?" You have minimal accountability. How does the interviewer know, after all, if you would really react in a given situation the way you say you would? In a behavioural interview, however, it is much more difficult to give responses that are untrue to your character. When you start to tell a behavioural story, the behavioural interview typically will pick it apart to try to get at the specific behaviours. The interviewer will probe further for more depth or detail such as, "What were you thinking of at that point?" or "Tell me more about your meeting with that person," or "Lead me through your decision process". If you have told a story that is anything but totally honest, your response will not help up through the barrage of probing questions.

Employers use the behavioural interview technique to evaluate a candidate's experiences and behaviours so that they can determine the applicant's potential for success. The interviewer identifies job-related experiences, behaviours, knowledge, skills and abilities that the company has decided are desirable in a particular position. Some of the characteristics that an employer looks for include:

1) Critical thinking

2) Being a self-starter

3) Willingness to learn

4) Willingness to travel

5) Self-confidence

6) Teamwork

7) Professionalism.

The employer then structures very pointed questions to elicit detailed responses aimed at determining if the candidate possesses the desired characteristics.

Behavioural interview questions can be used to identify skills in a variety of areas, including:

1) past job performance

2) oral and written communication

3) decision making

4) teamwork

5) flexibility

6) goal setting

7) time management

8) assertiveness

9) creativity

10) integrity

11) technical skills.

Outline the knowledge, strengths and experience that are necessary for the success of the job. With these attributes in mind, formulate questions that focus on each particular competency needed to perform the job. The objective is to frame questions which will elicit responses that reveal an applicants' qualities and character.

Behaviour-based questions invite the job applicant to tell a story. The theory behind behaviour-based interviewing is that by hearing about a job-seeker's past behaviour, the employer can predict his future behaviour.

Questions (often not even framed behaviour question) typically start out as, "Tell me about a time..." or "Describe a situation..." Many employers use a rating system to evaluate selected criteria during the interview.

The following are some examples of behaviourally-based questions:

1) Tell me about a time when you had to manage multiple projects and conflicting deadlines.

2) What did you do?

3) What was the result?

4) Give me an example of when you dealt with a difficult customer.

5) What happened?

6) What was the outcome?

7) Think about a time when you made a mistake in calculations.

8) What happened?

9) What was the result?

10) What accomplishment are you particularly proud of?

11) When did you handle a conflict with your boss, colleagues, or subordinates? Tell me about it.

12) Tell me about a situation that demonstrates your work habits.

13) Describe a time when you and your superior were in conflict. How was it resolved?

Semi-structured Interviews

Semi-structured interviews are also known as focused interviews. They are developed to combine advantages of structured and unstructured interviews, and involve use of additional questions.

This type of interview gives the researcher the opportunity to hear the participant talk about a particular aspect of his life or experience. The questions must be so framed as to trigger participants to talk.

It is important to take the interviewer identity into consideration to avoid bias, and important to familiarise with the respondent's cultural milieu and the status of 'the interview' within this milieu. An interview with a young person may invite to a more informal approach with an interviewer around the same age, and an interview with a middle-aged professional may invite to a more formal style.

This style of interview is one of the most widely used methods of data collection in qualitative research in psychology.

It is important that the interviewer is aware of linguistic variability, that is, it is important to understand the meaning of what the candidate says, for example, in that particular context. It is also important to establish a rapport between the interviewer and the candidate and observe ethical considerations; for example, in spite of a good atmosphere between the researcher and the candidate the interview should not abuse the informal ambience to make the candidate reveal more than he is comfortable with after the event.

The interview agenda should comprise a relatively small number of open-ended questions that allow the researcher to identify the candidate's own ideas and terms into the interview, so that questions become more relevant to the candidate. Careful reflections on what good questions are, and a good idea to restate the candidate's comments and integrate them in later questions in order to show that the interviewer is listening, are necessary. It is also good to express ignorance because a naïve interviewer encourages the candidate to 'state the obvious'. It is important that the questions are meaningful to the respondent.

Different kinds of questions can be used. Descriptive questions prompt the candidate to give a general account of 'what happened' or 'what it feels like to...", anecdotes, life histories, etc. Structural questions prompt the candidate to identify structures and meanings to use to make sense of the word; for example, "What does it mean to your life to suffer from AIDS?"

Contrast questions allow the candidate to make comparisons between events and experiences; for example, "Did you prefer being in that company or the other?"

Evaluative questions are about the candidate's feelings about someone or something; for example, "Did you feel afraid when the HIV test was taken?"

The semi-structured type of interview has more flexibility in the interview, while at the same time having the advantages of a structural approach. It allows for analysis in a variety of ways because it is compatible with many methods of data analysis. It is also easier to arrange than other forms of data collection, as it has few logistical difficulties to arrange a series of semi-structured interviews with a small number of participants than to design a longitudinal study.

Unstructured Interviews

In an unstructured interview, also known as indepth interviewing, researchers an elicit information in order to achieve a holistic understanding of the interviewee's point of view; it can also be used to explore interesting areas for further investigation. This type of interview involves asking informants open-ended questions, and probing, wherever necessary, to obtain a deemed to be useful by the interviewer. An indepth interviewing often involves qualitative data, it is also called qualitative interviewing.

This style of interview does not follow a fixed series of questions. The result is a more informal setting that often makes the applicant feel more at ease. However, the lack of structure may make it difficult for an interviewer to acquire all needed information, and adequately compare candidates.

The unstructured interview is more like a conversation. The interviewer works from a list of general topics, but has greater freedom to explore areas of interest. The interview allows full exploration of ideas and beliefs, that is, it is a more valid account of social life. It is flexible, and allows the interviewer to pursue interesting points.

But such a type of interview also has its negative aspect. It involves problems of reliability, replication and time costs. The candidate is too much in control.

An unstructured interview can be conducted in three ways: informal or conversational interview, general interview guide approach, and standardised open-end interview.

Conversational Interviews

The informal, conversational interview is more of a discussion where there are no predetermined set of questions. This style is chosen by the interviewer mainly because they can get more information from people as they tend to be more honest and open in a released atmosphere.

No predetermined questions are asked in order to remain as open and adaptable as possible to the candidate's nature and priorities. During the interview, the interviewer goes with the flow.

This type of interview resembles a chat during which the candidates may sometimes forget that they are being interviewed. Most of the questions will flow from the immediate context.

While all interviews are formal in some sense, it is quite common for the first part of the interview, at least, to be somewhat unstructured. The interviewer wants to get to know the candidate a little better to find out more about the person behind the resume. The interviewer will usually prepare a number of points of discussion based on the candidate's background, and ask questions designed to reveal more about him. The interview will proceed according to the leads that the candidate provides in his responses. It is important then for him to be proactive in this process.

This type of interview gives maximum flexibility to be able to pursue questioning in whatever direction appears to be appropriate. It requires an interviewer to be experienced and knowledgeable in the content area, and strong in interpersonal skills, since he will have considerable discretion in directing the interview.

Informal conversational interviews are useful for exploring interesting topics for investigation and are typical of ongoing participant observation fieldwork.

There are certain advantages and disadvantages in such a type of interview:

1) It is highly individualised and relevant to the individual.

2) It is likely to produce information or insights that the interviewer could not have anticipated.

3) It generates less systematic data that is difficult and time

consuming to classify and analyse.

4) Since different information is collected from different people, this kind of interview is not systematic or comprehensive and it can be very difficult and time consuming to analyse the data.

5) Data from such interviews can be difficult to compare because the questions that are asked may be unique each time.

6) This kind of interview allows for unanticipated comments and the interviewer can probe or ask follow-up questions.

7) It allows the candidate to respond quickly to individual differences and situational changes.

General Interview Guide Approach

This is commonly called the guided interview. The approach is intended to ensure that the same general rules of information are collected from each candidate. This provides more focus than the conversational approach to ensure that the same general areas of information are collected from each interviewee. This provides more focus than the conversational approach, but still allows a degree of freedom and adaptability in getting information from the interviewee.

When employing this approach for interviewing, a basic checklist is prepared to make sure that all relevant topics are covered. The interviewer is still free to explore, probe and ask questions deemed interesting to the researcher. The type of interview approach is useful for eliciting information about specific topics. It is useful as it allows for indepth probing while permitting the interviewer to keep the interview within the parameters traced out by the aim of the study.

Standardised Open-ended Interviews

An open-ended question is where candidates are free to choose how to answer the question, that is, they don't select 'yes' or 'no' or provide a numeric rating, etc. Researchers using this approach prepare a set of open-ended questions which are carefully worded and arranged for the purpose of minimising variation in the questions posed to the candidates. The same open-ended questions are asked to all candidates.

This approach facilitates faster interviews that can be more easily analysed and compared. In view of this, this method is often preferred for collecting interviewing data when two or more researchers are involved in the data collecting process. Although this method provides less flexibility for questions than the other two mentioned previously, probing is still possible, depending on the nature of the interview and the skills of the interviewers.

The wording of questions is very important. It should be open-ended. The candidates should be able to choose their own terms when answering questions.

Questions should be as neutral as possible. Avoid wording that might influence answers, for example, evocative, judgemental wording. Questions should be asked one at a time, and worded clearly. This includes knowing any terms particular to the programme or the candidates' culture.

Be careful asking 'why' questions. This type of question infers a cause-effect relationship that may not truly exist. These questions may also cause the candidates to feel defensive, for example, that they have to justify their response, which may inhibit their responses to this and future questions.

The advantage is that this type of interview makes sure questions are asked in the same way across a sample population by different interviewers. The weakness lies in the risk of losing important, unanticipated information.

Closed, Fixed-response Interviews

Here, all the candidates are asked the same questions, and asked to choose answers from among the same set of alternatives. Or, they are given questions inviting a brief answer, often just a 'yes' or 'no'. For example, "Did you fill in the application form yourself?" You can start the interview with closed questions like this, and also when you start any new line of questioning.

Closed questions allow the candidate to gradually warm up and be more relaxed. But watch your tone of voice as you gradually shift to open-ended questions, as you do not want to give the impression that you have cornered a victim for interrogation.

One-to-One Interviews

In this type of job interview, you are interviewed by one person, such as, by a manager, a senior executive, or an owner or proprietor of an organisation. The style of interview can vary from formal to relaxed, and will often reflect the personality of the interviewer. Whatever the style, you need to be mindful that the interviewer is assessing you as a future employee, and stay alert, positive and responsive to the questions asked.

This is the standard no-frills approach to interviewing. This is the form preferred by most candidates. It resembles more nearly a conversation, rather than the third-degree of the panel interview.

Anyone who has ever held a job of any sort is probably familiar with the format. First the candidate is screened over the phone or through an application form. Once he is selected for the interview, he is quickly led through a question and answer session to determine whether he is the right choice to fit into the company culture or mix. Success or failure are often based on such tenuous issues as whether the interviewer liked him or did the candidate use the word 'paradigm' correctly.

The goal of the candidate would be to build a rapport with the interviewer and successfully demonstrate an understanding of the company he is applying to, and the nature of the work he hopes to be undertaking.

A good interview feels like the candidate has just been making conversation with a new best friend, whereas a bad one feels like he has just been interrogated or grilled for an hour.

Every interviewer at different organisations has his own style, but there are certain routine questions that you can expect. It is a good idea for the candidate to know why the interviewer ask each question, what he is looking for, and the best possible way to answer it to make a good impression.

The informal conversation will focus on the candidate, his curriculum vitae, the role and company. A small or medium-sized company will generally conduct its interviews in this way, where the only people are the interviewer and the candidate. Generally this type of interview is far easier than a selection interview as the candidate only has to worry about impressing one person. That is not to say a one-to-one interview is not nerve wracking, it can be just as daunting as the others. The candidate should remember to keep calm, smile and stay positive. It has advantages for the interviewer too, for it allows one person to control the progress of the interview.

Two-on-one Interviews

The two-interviewer interview is often no more than a small panel interview. In this type of interview, the candidate is questioned by two interviewers, who will generally have worked out who will ask which questions, and in what order. While one may be sympathetic, the other may be conformational.

Such a method is somewhat more objective than the one-on-one type, as it allows for later discussion between the interviewers about the best candidate for the position. It is supposed to reveal the candidate's probable reaction to pressure in the workplace.

A somewhat extreme version of this type of interview is the 'stress' or 'pressure' interview, where applicants are subjected to rapid questioning, often in an abrupt or even hostile manner, to determine how well they can cope under pressure. This method is not common, and its use is generally limited to recruiting high-pressure positions, such as commission selling.

Panel/Committee Interviews

In this style of interview, you are interviewed by a panel of interviewers, sometimes each person that has a seat on the interview committee is representing a different department. They all have their own reason for being there, but the goal is to hire the best person for the job.

These interviews tend to be more formal, so hopefully this experience will not be your first interview ever. Often higher-level executives go through this process, but more and more companies are trying different formats to find what works best for them. You may be interviewed by whole panel of eight to ten people, or just three, two that ask questions and one that takes notes.

The panel interview is much used by employers such as the public service, universities, government establishments and research establishments. This has the advantage of bringing to bear the experience of a number of people, involving at least three, and often as many as seven, interviewers. At least one interviewer is an 'independent' whose role is to ensure that selection is not based by discriminatory practices, and to provide an external perspective to the interview process.

A panel interview can be the most daunting. Sitting in front of so many people rapidly firing questions at you can easily put even the most confident applicant on edge. This type of interview is normally associated with high position roles. The candidate attending one should ensure that he is fully prepared for the interview. He should not put off applying for a job that requires such an interview, as a company willing to have these many people spend time at an interview shows that the position is an important one, and how vital it is that they find the right candidate for the role.

Most people hate such an interview and find it a bit of an endurance test. To do well the candidate will need to identity the important figures on the panel, and which role each is fulfilling. The chairperson is easy to identity as he will generally make the introductions. The candidate will also need to identify the person whom he will be working for directly, and give him plenty of eye contact.

Companies using the committee format get a broader understanding of how the candidate will fit into their mix. Each interviewer will gain a different perspective on him. From the candidate's point of view, he gets to see the kinds of people he will be working with. Of all the interview types, this is the most dramatic and reliable.

The company gets to see how the candidate interacts with a cross-section of its staff.

Group Interviews

This type of interview is used to find a core set of applicants from a large number of people interested in the positions available. Normally located in a conference room within a hotel or company premises, one or two days are spent with other applicants undertaking presentations, group discussions and solving technical or business-related issues.

Focus group discussions are among the most widely used research tool, taking advantage of the interaction between a small group of people. The group interview pits one candidate against two or more interviewers. Oftentimes, one interviewer will assume a positive stance towards the candidate, one will be more ambivalent, while a third will be downright antagonistic.

Company representatives will mark the individual on various aspects during the event. It is important for the candidate to keep his personality in check by ensuring that he does not try to dominate, and not be too shy. Group participation skills are the key to a successful result.

The group recruitment method offers several advantages over conventional one-to-one interviewing, which is a very difficult method of recruiting the right person. It enables a number of people from the organisation to observe a number of job candidates, as they go through a series of specially designed activities. It also offers the recruiting organisation an excellent opportunity to present the company and the job in a very professional way, thus appealing to and attracting the best candidates. Also, the unsuccessful candidates leave the process with a very positive impression of the organisation and the experience as a whole.

Group selection also enables the best people to show themselves to be the best, often working on real job-related scenarios, which removes much of the guess work about people's true abilities. One-to-one interviews always favour the 'professional interviewee' types, who present very well, but then often actually fail to deliver.

Group selection activities are by far the most reliable way to see what people are really like, provided the process is carefully planned, managed and facilitated.

Here is an outline of the process:

1) Create/confirm job specification, job description, skill set, and person-profile.

2) Plan recruitment and induction schedule.

3) Create and place advertisement.

4) Shortlist applicants from written applications or curriculum vitae.

5) Write to candidates explaining the selection process, venue, date and time.

6) Plan the group selection day to include presentation to them by senior managers about the company and the role; psychometric tests; activities, tasks and syndicate work, and individual presentations; lunch; culminating in one-to-one interviews (usually three or four) involving final shortlisted candidates with senior managers on rotation.

7) Management review and decision. Candidates can be asked to leave and hear later or wait, depending on the situation.

8) Job offers, acceptance, reference checks, induction.

In small-group interviews, participants will respond to, and build on, what others in the group have said; a synergistic approach believed to generate more insightful information, and encourages discussion participants to give more candid answers.

Such groups are further characterised by the presence of a moderator and the use of a discussion guide. The moderator should stimulate discussion among group members rather than interview individual members, that is to say, every participant should be encouraged to express his views on each topic as well as respond to the views expressed by the other participants.

In order to put the participants at ease, the moderator will often start out by assuring everyone that there are no right or wrong answers, and that his feelings cannot be hurt by any views that are expressed since he does not work for the organisation for which the research is being conducted.

The advantages and disadvantages of group interviews are as follows:

1) It is relatively easy, and can be done quickly.

2) The social interaction in the group provides more free and complex answers.

3) The moderator or interviewer can ask for clarification.

4) It has high face validity.

5) It requires a skilled moderator, and it is difficult to assemble a group.

6) There may be problems as to whether the group represents a larger population or all the candidates selected for the discussions.

Telephone Interviews

A small number of organisations currently conduct telephone interviews as a first stage of selection to screen candidates for basic qualifications. These can range from a basic check to see whether a candidate matches the selection criteria. It is also an alternative when it is not practical to invite all out-of-area candidates to the office.

Smaller organisations, or organisations recruiting staff from a wide geographical base, may use an initial telephone interview as a screening device to cut down on the number of applicants for a position.

If prospective employer is heavily recruiting, this can be a way of saving time for you and the company. A telephone interview must be approached carefully as it is easy to be biased to the fact that the candidate is at home during the interview—normally, the process is informal, but you must ensure that you treat it as part of the interviewing process. The list of questions that you prepare can be standardised.

Telephone interviews can be challenging because it is more difficult to gain rapport for a candidate with the interviewer as the latter cannot see the enthusiastic or professional appearance of the former, nor can the candidate see the interviewer's, non-verbal reactions and cues. This places all the weight on the candidates phone manners, clarity of speech, voice tone and content of his answers. Clarity of speech, variation of tone in the voice, and good listening skills are therefore very important.

Use the telephone interview to:

1) Fill in the missing information on the candidate's resume.

2) Question the candidate to determine his level of interest.

3) Get a feeling for the candidate's communication skills.

4) Ask some questions to get a sense of the candidate's technical qualifications.

5) Decide whether to invite the candidate for a personal interview.

This type of interview is becoming more common now, especially for minimising expenses. While the candidate can have his notes there to refer to, he does not have the benefit of positive body language to make the connection with the interviewer.

Basically, a telephone interview is a stepping stone to another interview.

Videoconferencing Interviews

Sometimes employers interview prospective employees through videoconferencing. Interviewing applicants by videoconferencing rather than flying them from various places can save money for companies. This technological choice in interviewing is becoming increasingly popular in the West.

Interviews via video links deprive the candidate and the interviewer of the opportunity to fully read the body language. There the candidates need to stay on the point but be concise, as he may not be able to tell if the interviewer is getting bored.

Selection Interviews

The selection interview is less formal than the ranking interview. Usually, the selection interview is a one-to-one meeting: the interviewer and the interviewee. If the panel interview is used for the actual selection process, the procedures adopted for the ranking interview should be followed.

The questions used in the selection interview generally meet the same requirements as the questions for the ranking interview. You should be well prepared. You should review the position description, the job analysis, and available information about the employee.

From the job analysis, the questions and the rating scale should be developed. In the selection interview, questions about experience/training that were covered in the preliminary rounds may be asked if the question is about the quality of experience. For example, the preliminary analysis matches certain skills pertaining to the position and to the skills the candidate presently possesses; the selecting official should interview those candidates in order to further evaluate the candidate's quality of experience related to the skill matched up with in the preliminary rounds. It is useful to have a scale by which candidates' responses are evaluated. This scale would show 'best' response, 'good' response and 'minimum' response. This would be used as documenting how you evaluated each candidate. It may be easier to assign points to these responses as shown below:

Best : 10 points

Good : 5 points

Minimum : 2 points

The selection interview should be conducted using the same guidelines as pointed out in the ranking interview:

1) Make the candidate comfortable.
2) Introduce the interviewer (tell a little about yourself).
3) Clarify questions, if needed.
4) Spend about equal amounts of time with each candidate.
5) Do not 'test' the candidate.
6) Allow the candidate to ask questions.
7) Indicate when the candidate will know the results of the interview.

The selection type of interview is useful in establishing very quickly the right type of candidates for the company. Generally you ask the candidates about themselves, and why they want to work for your company and in the role they are applying for. A large number of candidates may be weeded out during this process, and it is important to make a good impression to get on the second interview short-list. The interviewer would normally be from the personnel department, although if the role is of a technical or skilled nature, the candidate will be asked specific questions to assess his skill – set by someone else who knows about the role.

Internal or Promotion Interviews

An internal interview occurs when a candidate interviews for a new position or promotion within the company where he already works.

At promotion interviews, interviewers particularly expect to hear the applicant's practical and cost-effective ideas and plans for the new job. He should be able to demonstrate how well he understands the business and the organisation. If appropriate, his ideas can be fresh and innovative, especially if you, as the interviewer, are innovative and creative yourself, but he must above all be able to demonstrate a clear grasp of 'cause and effect' and the importance of achieving a suitable return on effort or investment.

Promotion almost always involves having responsibility for making decisions about the use of time and resources. You need to be convinced that the candidate understands how to handle this responsibility to identify priorities, to focus effort in the right direction, to manage efforts productively as if he was using his own money.

Demonstrating clear knowledge and interpretation of policies, processes, rules, standards, and a firm and diplomatic style when supervising others, is crucial for promotion into most first line management or supervisory roles.

Demonstrating an ability to plan, organise and achieve effective implementation of plans, changes and objectives is crucial for promotion into most middle management positions.

Demonstrating huge personal commitment and enthusiasm, together with complete and utter loyalty to one's boss and the organisation, are always essential factors for successful promotion interviews. Loyalty and commitment are essential. You must be able to trust the candidate to the extent that you will stake your reputation on his commitment and ability.

The ability to adopt and be flexible as priorities and circumstances change around the candidates is also essential for promotion into most supervisory and management roles.

E-mail Interviews

E-mail interviews may be used when conducting an interview in person, or contacting via telephone. It is appropriate due to location, schedule conflict, or different time zones. Interviewers make phone calls to contact or interview people.

E-mail interviews give quick results and are relatively inexpensive. But there are problems to establish a proper sampling frame, and this kind of contact may have cultural limitations.

Questionnaires

This is in reality a survey that is administered in person. Since all the participants are asked the same questions, the answers of one respondent can easily be compared to those of another.

The questionnaire is superior to a written survey in that the interviewer can observe the body language of the candidates, and record emphasis and intonation.

Stress Interviews

Some companies view the stress interview as a useful way of guaging a person's capabilities at handling stressful situations.

Unless a candidate is a masochist who thrives on pain and likes stress because it makes him feel alive, chances are the stress interview is going to do just that—stress him out, of course. Some jobs demand that a candidate can cope with stress. Pilots, police officers and talk show hosts are careers where stress is to be expected.

While it is no secret that most job applicants view employment interviews as stressful, many are not aware that there is an intentionally designed and somewhat unusual type of selection interview, called a 'stress interview'. The stress approach can be in the form of questions or statements. A mild stress question may be, "With your lack of relevant experience, what makes you think you can do this job?" or medium stress, "You seem too much timid to handle these responsibilities" or major stress, "That is the worst answer we have heard from any of the candidates."

The stress could be presented in a situation or disguised in the interviewer's behaviour, such as an unsmiling greeting, protracted silence after hearing the candidate's answer to a particular question or a confrontational or argumentative attitude.

In stress interviews, if the interviewer snaps at a candidate, or becomes argumentative, the candidate may feel as through he has just walked into a battlefield, but he should not take the attempt to rile him personally. Hitting the interviewer and crying are unlikely to get him the job. He should keep the interview on track, and not be swayed by long pauses or argumentative outbursts.

Stress approaches may include rapid-fire questioning, criticism of the candidate's interview or past work performance, silence in the beginning or following an answer to a question asked of the candidate, unclear instructions, or being confronted by the interviewer.

It is important for job seekers to keep in mind that it is one's reaction—how one handles stressful, unexpected questions and/or the interviewer's surprising behaviour that is observed and assessed by the interviewer, not necessarily the answer.

Candidates should not take the stress tactics personally. Their reactions should be evaluated relative to the genuine demands of the work, and 'grace under fire' is the key to handling this unusual situation.

Actually, many hiring professionals agree that a full interview using a stress approach is seldom used or appropriate these days because heavy- handed stress tactics do not fit well with the relaxed and welcoming interview atmosphere that some organisations, especially in the West, attempt to create for candidates.

As a leading group publisher in Canada says, "Whether we use stress tactics or not depends totally on the expectations of the job. If we are hiring creative staff, we don't use it. However, if we are hiring for sales and marketing, we do ask stress questions and we create a bit of an unexpected atmosphere. We are not out to create tremendous stress as that is not productive. We just want to see how the person reacts and we expect honesty in answers... We use a combination of waiting and silence. If we are interviewing for a sales and marketing position, we will have an applicant wait about 10 minutes, and then bring the person into the interview room. We say hello, smile and then — silence .. "Our goal is to see if the candidate will initiate the conversation". It can even be small talk – as long as they start the conversation. On the job, a salesperson has to demonstrate composure and control to strike up a friendly conversation with a client. The stress tactic tells us if the person can do that.

Some interviewers use the stress tactic at the end of the interview as well. They know that when they ask about 'weaknesses' they get a rehearsed answer, but by adding the stress following question, "Tell me more about your weaknesses," they are likely to get an honest and unrehearsed answer.

Chronological Interviews

This is a traditional style of interview, based firmly on your written application. It asks you to explain what you have written on your form. It is predictable, and includes questions like:

1) How did you fare in the final year of your school?

2) What led you to study Mathematics at the university?

3) Why are you interested in applying for the present job?

4) How do you see your career developing with our organisation?

Screening Interviews

Screening interviews are useful in short-listing candidates for group selections. For a senior job group selection, screening interviews and psychometric assessments are recommended to shortlist candidates.

Many times screening is done over the phone, via an application form or through testing. The idea is to minimise the amount of time a company wastes interviewing unqualified candidates. Interviewers will often be less prepared than normal because they are merely gauging whether you are worth spending more time researching. The interviewer will often work straight off your resume, looking for inconsistencies.

Clinical Interviews

These are generally used by doctors, dentists, psychologists, etc., to gather personal information. Questions do not usually follow a pre-set order.

The advantages of the informal, non-directive or unstructured interview are that people speak more freely plus truthfully about themselves, and the interview may give valuable information about the person's mental state.

Lunch Interviews

These are conducted when business or other conditions prevent a normal interview situation. Perhaps, they are a screening tool, or more likely, an invitation to a company who has already decided they want to hire the candidate.

Case Interviews

A case interview is a variation on behavioural interview, and is now being used by management consultants, law firms, social work and counselling organisations, and police departments. This method is used by employers whose recruitment requirements emphasises understanding the thought processes of job applicants.

Case interviews will present to the candidate a series of facts relating to a work situation, and such interviews are designed to observe how he analyses, concludes and acts to recommend actions to be taken. His task in such interviews is to become the professional, make further enquiries to clarify the facts, develop and present a framework for thinking about the issues, and then work within the framework of the situation (or scenario) to come to conclusions. Case questions can relate to business operations or business strategy.

Research Method

Employers should always follow up and check successful job interview candidate's references. Not to do so is irresponsible, especially if recruiting for jobs which carry serious responsibilities, such as working with children, disabled people, sensitive data money, valuables, etc. He must inform or ask permission from the candidates prior to checking their references.

The extent and depth to which references should be checked depend on the situation and the references given by the job applicant. The employer should certainly make job offers conditional to satisfactory checking of references, and if he is not happy about the references, provided, then he must ask for others.

Checking references can be a very sensitive area, so care needs to be used. Many referees will not be comfortable providing personal information about a person, not least due to fear of defaming someone and the liabilities concerned.

Care must be taken to interpret carefully any personal comments which might stem from personality clash. The employer must concentrate on facts with evidenced examples rather than opinions. References should definitely be checked concerning job-critical areas, as should any areas of suspicion or doubt that cannot be resolved or proven for sure at the interview.

And for everyone, irrespective of satisfaction with interview answers, it is important to check some basic facts with past employers to ensure that the candidate has not been telling a pack of lies.

The possible areas to check are:

1) Curriculum vitae, career history, dates, salaries

2) Qualifications and training

3) Personal details, age, etc.

4) Claims about achievements and performance in past jobs

5) Personality and relationships at work

6) Domestic and financial situation.

Competence-based Interviews

Many employers use a structured criteria-based interview to ensure a fairer or more objective assessment of applicants. They will have decided on the selection criteria for each job, and will then ask each candidate similar questions to supply evidence to determine whether or not they have the skills to do the job effectively. Applicants are marked on a set scale, according to how well they have demonstrated that they have the competencies required.

The competence-based interview is demanding and requires careful thought. For example, if the job requires the candidate to work closely with others to achieve an objective, the questions might be:

1) Tell me about an occasion when you have worked well in a group.

2) What was your personal contribution?

3) Did you have to convince others of your viewpoint? How did you persuade them?

4) Did you encounter any difficulties? How did you deal with them?

5) Were you satisfied with the outcome?

6) Was it successful? What would you change to make it more successful next time?

In this style of interview, questions are more detailed and probing than in the traditional approach. The candidate will need evidence, ranging from the general through to very specific. It is likely that the interviewer will challenge him on his opinions to test how well formulated they are. The candidate must make sure to prepare several examples from different activities to illustrate each criterion.

Recording and Transcription of Interviews

In order to carry out a full analysis of the data, it is necessary to audio record or video record, and transcribe the interview. Most qualitative methods of analysis require that the material is transcribed verbatim, or near about it. Taking notes during the interview may interfere with eye contact and non-verbal communication, so it distracts the interviewer. However, taping the interview may also affect what is being said, because participants are not entirely comfortable and relaxed in the presence of tape or video recorder. It is important that the interviewer explains why the recording is being made, and how it is going to be used. It is also a good idea to offer the candidate a copy of the transcript, if possible.

If the interview is being recorded, the interviewer needs to make sure that the recorder is placed in a position where it will record clearly, and that the interviewer has eye contact with the candidate. The recorder should be working so that the interview is not spoiled by bad technique.

Second Interview

A second interview occurs when the first round of interview has whittled the prospective candidates down to a few that are suitable for the position. Sometimes a second interview may be required for technical, specialist or senior positions so that an interview with the appropriate skills or seniority can finalise the decision on the candidates. For certain jobs a decision will be made to offer the job after the second interview. Recruitments for senior positions may proceed to third interviews. This can lead on to discussing salary, benefits, package, the role and the department.

Second interview questions should be deep and probing about the candidate and the candidate's approach to work. The questions should concern detailed and testing examples and scenarios specific to the particular job, asking how the candidate would deal with them. This is to discover as reliably as possible, how the candidate would approach the job, and what type of persons they are—the interviewer needs to be sure they will get on with the candidates and that they will fit in well.

The interviewer should also probe the type of management that the candidate responds to and does not, and how the candidate would work with other people and departments, giving specific examples and scenarios.

Tests and practical exercises using actual work material or examples can be used, which enable a practical assessment of the candidate's real style, ability, knowledge and experience.

The candidates can be asked to prepare and give a short presentation about themselves, or how they would approach the job or a particular challenge. This could involve the use of certain equipment and materials, particularly if such ability is to be required in the job.

The interviewer should also try to get to know more about the candidate as a person—to be as sure as possible that this is the right person for the situation. The interview approach should be probing and gaining practical evidence of suitability.

A good second interview should establish as reliably as possible the candidate's suitability and ability for the specific needs of the job, which includes the work, relationships, aspirations and personal background.

There is nothing wrong in the candidate asking the organisation prior to the interview what to plan and prepare for in the second interview. Interviewers should regard this as a positive sign, and it may help the candidate to give some clear information on what to expect and prepare for.

Certain senior job recruitments will involve a lunch or dinner so that the interviewer and other senior members or executives can see the candidate in a relaxed mood. This is an excellent way to discover more about the personality of an applicant.

Group selection is a very good alternative to conventional one-to-one interviews after the first interview stage. Group selection puts all the candidates and tasks, which can then be observed by a panel of interviewers.

All types of transcription constitute a form of translation of the spoken word into something else, and an interview transcription can never be the mirror image of the interview.

Different ways can be used in transcription of an interview, that is, if you are interested in the subtleties of communicative interaction between interviewer and interviewee, you must transcribe the words as well as the way in which they are spoken. This means including pauses, interruptions, intonation, volume of speech and so on. These various features are represented by the signs of the transcription notation.

Detailed description is required for conversation analysis , and some types of discursive analysis. If you are interested only in the content of the interview, you need not transcribe non-linguistic features of the interview. In this case, it is sufficient to transcribe what is being said, that is, the words alone. This would be appropriate for grounded theory analysis. However , even here it is important to decide what to include or if you want to 'tidy up' the transcript. It all depends on what you want to use the transcript for. So basically the decision about what type of transcription to use depends upon the research question and the method of analysis chosen.

Committee Interviews

Companies using the committee format require you to interview a succession of people inside the company. While this process may be exhausting for the candidate (having to say , "I would really like to work for your company because ....."five times can become tiresome), it is a great way for the company to get a broader understanding of how the candidate will fit into its mix. Each interviewer will gain a different perspective on him. From the candidate's point of view, he gets to see the kinds of people he will be working with (or not, if he thinks you are all idiots!) and don't have to worry about the interview because one interviewer does not take to him. Of all the interview types, this is the most democratic and reliable.

While the company's goal is to get to see how the candidate interacts with a cross-section of its staff, the candidate's goal is to keep going from one interview to the next, and maintain his composure.

4

The Interview Room

It is always appreciated if the setting in the interview room is as comfortable as possible for both the interviewer and the candidate.

Check that there is no incoming calls to disturb the interview, and try to keep other external interruptions to a minimum.

Make sure that the desk is tidy without clearing it. A totally clear desk does not give a feel of reality, and is in danger of evoking the interrogation room, thus daunting an already apprehensive candidate.

The lighting and seating need careful attention. Make sure that the light from your desk lamp does not focus directly into the candidate's face. Also remember not to sit with your back to an open window whereby the poor candidate has to endure the glare of direct sunlight while looking at you in shadow. This prevents him from having eye contact with you, or observing what impression he is making on you.

You may decide to have the usual procedure of interviewing across a desk or table, but this often results as a barrier rather than a channel when it comes to studying body language or conveying ideas.

Instead, it would be better to position two chairs a few feet apart at right angles to each other. Have comfortable office chairs rather than armchairs or sofas. If you feel that this arrangement looks inadequate, place a low coffee table in front of the chairs. This will prove useful if either of you has any paperwork to handle.

Finally, ensure that there is a clock on a wall or on your desk which you can clearly see, so that you do not have to keep glancing frequently at your watch.

5

The Interviewer's Behaviour

Interviews are stressful enough. So it is a good idea to create a more relaxed and calm atmosphere where the candidate can drop his guard a little — this will reveal more of the real person. If there is a sofa in your office, use that rather than an across-the-desk interview. Or if you have access to an informal meeting area, that will do just as well, as long as you have some privacy from inquisitive people and a lot of interruptions.

When opening the interview, it is most important to put the candidate at ease. Small talk is a good way to begin building a rapport between yourself and the candidate. In particular, you must reassure them that the interview is not a test, and that they are not being judged in any way. Also, provide a description of the interview format.

In any interview that you conduct, you have the primary duty to be an effective listener. This means that not only do you absorb and analyse the information offered by the interviewee, but also penetrate into the thoughts and feelings behind the information. You have to be alert and watchful as this will help you to learn a great deal from the candidate's tone of voice, body language, and from eye contact and facial expression.

You must also have to use these same devices to assure the candidate that you are listening carefully, and to coax him to continue.

Build the initial rapport with the candidate. Be ready with a warm and friendly welcome. One of the greatest factors in influencing someone is the welcome you give them in the crucial first five minutes of a meeting.

You must speak clearly, informally and openly as an interviewer. The candidate will reciprocate in a likewise manner. Maintain eye contact, but do not stare or glare too piercingly.

Do not hunch or slouch, but sit in a reasonably relaxed position. Take care of your gestures; avoid covering your mouth with your hand, frowning down your nose, etc. Instead, show your interest by being attentive, nodding your head, murmuring 'hmm' or 'I see'. This will put the candidate at ease, allowing him to talk freely and expansively.

During the interview, you must be careful not to ask closed questions which would limit the input by the candidate. Closed questions are those which can be answered quickly and succinctly by the candidate without providing any context or background to you. Open ended questions which place fewer constraints upon the candidate's responses are more desirable. These are useful to gain an appreciation of the scope of the problem domain.

You must practise active listening to reassure the candidate that his input is appreciated and understood. As well, care must be taken to avoid using words and expressions with negative emotional connotations for the subject. Acceptance cues are also important for drawing requirements from the subject. These include a welcoming posture, appropriate eye contact, and polite manners. Restatement of the candidate's comments in your own words is also an effective way of checking your interpretation and indicating your continued interest.

Sometimes there may be long pauses or lull in conversation. Don't feel that you should quickly try to break the silence. This will only result in the candidate becoming jittery, for probably he was just taking thought before replying. In case the pause turns awkward with the candidate showing signs of freezing up, you can gently repeat the question, or rephrase it slightly so that the candidate has a more accessible approach.

Generally, the candidate should be doing all the talking. Only a fifth or sixth of the conversation should be your input.

Many interviewers like to use a video or tape recorder. If you are expected to use it, make sure you are familiar with the equipment. Don't forget to reassure the candidate that this is normal procedure.

Most interviewers take notes while interviewing. Care must be taken through to see that your writing does not distract you from what the candidate is saying. Do the note taking openly; let the candidate not think that you are taking them down surreptiously. If necessary, explain that you need to pause for a moment to jot down a few points. Then resume eye contact and resume the conversation.

You may have to deal with your own prejudices both while conducting the interview and in passing judgement afterwards. Most of us have preconceived ideas and predispositions when it comes to strangers—anything from out-and-out sexism, to a vague distrust of beards. Instead of just pushing to one side such attitudes, you should first acknowledge any such attitudes openly to yourself, adjust that your judgement may be affected, and make special allowance for them.

Do not place too much emphasis on first impressions, which will only confirm your prejudices. Look beyond the smart suit and classy voice on the one hand, or the beard and regional accent on the other.

It is quite likely that you may fail to realise that there may be tension and artificiality in the interview setting. It would be unjustified to imagine that a person appearing nervous or reticent during an interview is likely to remain so once employed in a familiar workplace.

You may be biased in favour of those whose values and interests are similar to your own. You might take a liking to the candidate and have a good rapport with him, but let that not tempt you to overlook his inadequacies. The right person for the job is not necessarily the one you get on best with.

6

Conducting the Interview

Interviewing to many people is simply an extension of having a personal conversation. In fact, it is much more challenging, and requires development of skills far beyond those used in personal lives. Most of us, in conversations, rarely listen as carefully as is required in an interview situation. While the other person is talking in a personal conversation most of us are thinking of what we will say when it is our turn. In interviews it is crucial to not only hear what the other person is saying, but to thoroughly understand their meaning. This requires a concentration level much greater than that used in casual discussions.

An interview should be a controlled conversation, guided and controlled by the interviewer. Decide how long you want to allow for the interview, and try to keep to the time you set. Make sure that you meet and greet the candidates properly, to make notes and digest what you have learned.

Ensure the interview is conducted in private, and that there are no interruptions, either by telephone or person.

Arrange the interview room so that you can sit and talk naturally, and write, if necessary, but ideally without barriers, like a big desk between you.

Interviews are stressful enough. So it is a good idea to create a more relaxed atmosphere where the interviewees can drop their guard a little. This will reveal more of the real person. If there are comfortable chairs, use them or even the sofa, or settee. Or if you have access to an informal meeting area, that will do just as well as long as you have some privacy from prying ears.

Start by welcoming the candidate, and putting him at ease with some friendly chat. Remember, it is stressful for the candidate, so don't make it any worse by being very formal. Greet him in a friendly but business-like way, for you are the host and he is your guest.

Forget power plays like sitting in a higher seat or using an iron-grip handshake to intimidate the candidate. It is more professional and productive to be openly welcoming, and to spend the first few minutes getting to know the candidate with small talk. A question about the candidate's journey or the weather will do. Try to put him at ease from the start. One thing you must not do is to pry deeply into the person's private life.

Explain the interview process and the purpose of the interview. You can tell the candidate what will happen, who they will see, whether there will be tests, etc.

You can help the candidate relax and talk more openly by showing interest during the interview through your posture and expressions—nodding in agreement, smiling and maintaining good eye contact.

Address the terms of confidentiality. Tell the candidate that you will treat as confidential everything said in the interview.

Explain the format of the interview. Give an outline of the topics you want to cover. Explain the type of interview you are about to conduct, and its nature. If you want them to ask questions, specify if they are to do so as they have them or wait until the end of the interview.

Indicate how long the interview may last. Tell them how to get in touch with you later, if they want to. Ask them if they have any questions before you both get started with the interview.

Don't count on your memory to recall their answers. Ask for permission to record the interview, or bring along someone to take notes. Occasionally, verify if the tape recorder is working.

Begin by explaining clearly and concisely the general details of the organisation and the role.

Communicate well during the interview. Ask one question at a time. Ask open-ended questions—how, why, tell me, what, and to a lesser extent, where, when, which, to get the candidate talking. Direct questions about living arrangements, partner's employment, age, number of children, and plans for marriage should be strictly off limits. Asking these and other private questions could risk a potential equal opportunities law suit from applicants that have been turned down.

You should be in control of the interview at all times. It is your responsibility as the interviewer to direct the course of the discussion. You do this by asking the right kind of questions. They should be focused enough to get specific information that you need to know but open enough to let the interviewee expand on the subject. To ensure smooth progress, you should prepare a set of topics beforehand, and a list of clear questions based on these topics.

Listen to the way the questions are answered as much as the answers themselves. The best interviewee will only talk for about 20, 30 per cent of the interview, and invest the rest of the time listening actively for how the candidate answers the questions. The best way to achieve this is by using open-ended questions. Be careful not to ask closed questions which would limit the candidate's input. Closed questions are those which can be answered quickly and spontaneously by the user without providing any background or context to the interviewer. Hence open-ended questions which place fewer constraints upon the candidate's responses are more desirable. These are useful to gain an appreciation of the scope of the problem domain.

Control the interview. Practice techniques which allow you to open up uncommunicative candidates and direct talkative ones. The use of open questions for the former, and careful direction of the second are skills worth developing.

Avoid asking more than one question at a time. It will be difficult for the candidate to remember them all, and to know which one to answer first.

If you are taking notes during the interview, explain to the candidate what you are doing, and keep them brief so that you don't break the flow. You can then go back over them immediately after the interview to record thoughts and facts.

Once you have explained to the candidate what they need to know about the job and the company, ask if they have any questions.

Design the interview to test the candidate in a number of different ways. Test their on-the-job skills. The more realistic the tests to the actual job, the more valuable the information you will receive on the candidates' ability to perform to the required standard. If you have to interview many candidates you may want to make this a test they can perform in their own time prior to the interview, but ensure you give them sufficient notice.

Let the candidate open up to get his answers flowing, but if he starts to waffle move on to the next question.

During any conversation, most of the communication (above 90 per cent) is non-verbal. In fact, 55 per cent of communication is purely facial, with other messages coming from body movements, gestures and patterns of speech. Nervous gestures like adjusting clothing or fiddling with fingers are understandable given the situation. What you should be looking for are indications that the candidate may not be being straight with you:

1) Face touching or playing with hair can be a sign that he is hiding something.

2) Averting eyes, touching the mouth and shifting uncomfortably are indications that he is lying.

3) Looking away or hesitating before or while speaking indicates that he is unsure of what he is saying.

4) Excessive fidgeting shows boredom and restlessness.

There are also positive signs to look for:

1) Leaning forward, opened arms and nodding are signs of eagerness.

2) Head tilted to one side, constant eye contact nodding and verbal acknowledgment show that he is positively listening to what you are saying. Listening is a skill.

A great part of the skill of interviewing is to reassure the candidate that you are actively listening to what he has to tell you. This will make him feel more relaxed, comfortable and open to revealing his true self. The interviewer must practice active listening to reassure the candidate that his input is appreciated and understood. As well, care must be taken to avoid using words and expressions that make the candidate uncomfortable.

Acceptance cues are also important for drawing requirements from the candidate. These include a welcoming gesture, appropriate eye contact, and polite manner. Repeating the candidate's comments in one's own words is also an effective way of checking your interpretation, and indicating your continued interest.

Note-taking should not be allowed to detract from your personal interaction with the candidate. Audio and video are generally poor tools for interviewing, but they can work in certain situations.

Attempt to remain as neutral as possible, that is, don't show strong emotional reactions to a candidate's responses. Encourage responses with occasional nods of the head, hmm, etc.

Don't lose control of the interview. This can occur when the candidate strays to another topic, take so long to answer a question that time begins to run out, or even begin asking questions to the interviewer. High pressure rarely exposes hidden issues, while calm, relaxed, gentle, clever questions do.

When evaluating an individual's ability to perform technical or physical skills, you may wonder if it is wise to have the individual take a test of some sort. Unfortunately, tests can be legally problematic unless they have been determined to be both reliable and internally valid.

That does not unilaterally prohibit you from asking applicants to demonstrate how they would perform certain tasks. A demonstration is different than a test in that it does not have a passing or failing score or cut off. It just provides you with a piece of information you can use in considering the applicants. However, you should exercise caution even in asking candidates to demonstrate skills. First, if you ask one candidate, you must ask all of them. Second, you must only ask individuals to demonstrate skills that represent essential functions of the job.

Guidelines for Efficient Interviews

1) Create the right environment.

2) Establish rapport early.

3) Allow adequate time for the candidate to respond.

4) Start off on a positive note.

5) Use open-ended questions.

6) Ask specific job-related questions.

7) Let the other person do most of the talking.

8) Question tactfully.

9) Maintain positive eye contact.

10) Try and mirror the candidate's body posture and talking speed.

11) Encourage him to continue when you want more information.

12) Account for all time.

13) Look for contrary evidence.

14) Judge only by history.

15) Downplay the negative information.

16) Give the candidate credit where credit is due.

17) Control the interview.

18) Clarify the information the candidate gives you.

19) Evaluate the information.

20) Make each interview important.

21) Be sensitive to cultural differences.

22) Do be specific in questioning.

23) Do listen! Don't talk!

24) Do take notes, especially if any candidate will be interviewed.

25) Do invite the candidate to ask questions and discuss relevant topics.

26) Ensure there are no interruptions. Hold all calls and conduct the interview where you cannot see the office's day-to-day operations.

27) Watch the candidate's body language when he is answering questions.

28) Refrain from interrupting.

In his book, *The interviewer's Pocketbook*, John Townsend has tips for what makes interviewers better listeners :

1) Maintain positive eye contact.

2) Try and mirror the candidates body posture and talking speed.

3) Encourage him to continue when you want more information.

4) Paraphrase regularly what he is saying.

5) Clarify the information he gives you.

Give regular feedback indicating how you feel about his responses to his questions.

7

Questioning the Interviewee

Every job interviewee, if the job seeker is lucky, gets to the stage of an interview. What he does then controls whether or not he gets an offer. The resume gets him in the door, but whether he leaves as a job seeker or employee depends on how he conducts himself during the interview.

Individuals vary in the ability to articulate their thoughts and ideas. With good questioning techniques, you will be more able to facilitate the candidate's accounts, and to obtain quality data from him.

The first point to remember while interviewing the candidate is to ask clear questions. Many of the meanings which are clear to one will be relatively opaque to another, even when the intention is genuine communication. Accordingly, it is important to use words that make sense to the candidate, words that are sensitive to his context and worldview. To enhance their comprehensibility to the candidate, questions should be easy to understand, short, and devoid of jargon.

Always ask single questions. Some interviewers often put several questions together and ask them all as one. You should ask one question at a time. This will eliminate any unnecessary burden of interpretation on the candidate.

Ask fully open-ended questions. Truly open-ended questions do not predetermine the answers and allow room for the candidates to respond in their own terms. For example, "What do you think about your English?" or "How do you feel about the method of English teaching in your country" or "What is your opinion of English lessons in India?"

It is useful to ask questions about experience or behaviour before asking questions about opinions or feelings as this helps establish a context for the candidates to express the latter. For example, ask "What happened?" before "How do you feel now?"

Sequence the questions. This refers to a special kind of questioning technique called 'funneling' which means asking from general to specific, from broad to narrow.

Probe and have follow-up questions. The purpose of probing is to deepen the response to a question, to increase the richness of the data being opined, and to give cues to the candidate about the level of response that is desired. This can be done through direct questioning of what has been said, for example, "Could you say something more about that? Or "Can you give a more detailed description of what happened?" or "Do you have further examples of this?" Alternatively, a mere nod or 'mm' or just a pause can indicate to the candidate to go on with the description. Repeating significant words of an answer can lead to further elaboration.

Interpret the questions correctly. All through the interview, you should clarify and extend the meanings of the candidate's statements to avoid misinterpretations on their part. You may use questions like, "Is it correct that you feel that...? or"Does the expression...   cover what you have just expressed? "to allow the candidates to confirm or disconfirm what has been interpreted by you.

Avoid all sensitive questions. It is advisable to avoid deep questions which may irritate the candidate, possibly resulting in an interruption of the interview. He may well feel uneasy, and adopt avoidance tactics if the questioning is too deep.

Encourage a free rein but maintain control. You should be prepared to let the candidates 'travel' wherever they like, but a rough checklist of ideas or areas you want to explore is useful. A proficient interviewer should be always in control of a conversation which they guide and bend to the service of their research interest.

Establish a good rapport. This can be achieved by, for example, respecting the candidates' opinions, supporting their feelings or recognising their responses. This can also be shown by the tone of your voice, expressions or even gestures. In addition, a good contact is established by attentive listening, with you showing interest, understanding and respect for what the candidates say. A good interview allows candidates to finish what they are saying, lets them proceed at their rate of thinking and speaking.

An employer needs to follow these basic rules while conducting interviews :

1) Only ask questions related to the employment being sought.

2) Avoid leading questions, and questions that require a simple 'yes' or 'no' answer.

3) Watch the candidate's body language when answering questions.

4) Refrain from interrupting.

At the interview, you should brief the candidate as to the nature or purpose of the interview, being as can did as possible without biasing responses, and make him feel at ease. You should explain the manner in which you will be recording responses, and if you plan to tape record, you must inform him. At all times, you must remember that you are a data collection instrument and try not to let your biases, opinions or curiosity affect your behaviour.

Six kinds of questions can be asked. You can ask questions about:

1) behaviours—about what the candidate has done or is doing.

2) opinions/values—about what he thinks regarding a particular topic.

3) feelings—note that candidates sometimes respond with 'I think…'. So be careful to note that you are looking for feelings.

4) knowledge—to get facts about a topic.

5) sensory—about what people have seen, touched, heard, tasted or smelled.

6) background/demographics—standard background questions, such as age, education, etc.

Note that the above questions can be asked in terms of past, present or future.

The following sequence of questions can be useful for you as an interviewer:

1) Get the candidates involved in the interview as soon as possible.

2) Before asking about controversial matters, such as feelings and conclusions, first ask about some facts. With this approach the candidates can more easily engage in the interview before warning up to more personal matters.

3) Intersperse fact-based questions throughout the interview to avoid long lists of fact-based questions at one go, which tends to leave the candidates disengaged.

4) Ask questions about the present before questions about the past or future. It is usually easier for them to talk about the present, and then work into the past or future.

5) The last questions might be to allow the candidates to provide any other information they prefer to add, and their impressions of the interview.

Interviewers who are not yet using the behavioural style interview process generally use the traditional style. They will ask the candidates about their educational background, past work experience, extra curricular activities, and outside interests and activities.

Almost all interview questions asked in the traditional style can be boiled down to their base essence. When that is done, most questions give you indepth information about:

1) CAN you do the job?

2) WILL you do the job?

3) Do you FIT into my organisation?

They are, therefore, CAN, WILL or FIT questions. A list of typical questions follows.

CAN Type Questions

1) What are your greatest strengths and weaknesses?

2) How has your education prepared you for a career?

3) Why should I hire you?

4) What qualifications do you have that will make you successful in your job?

5) What relationship should exist between a supervisor and subordinate?

6) Describe your most rewarding educational experience?

7) Why did you select your college or university?

8) What led you to choose your field of major study?

9) What college subjects did you like best? Why?

10) If you could do so, how would you plan your academic study differently? Why?

11) What changes would you make in your college? Why?

12) What major problems have you encountered in your work area? How did you deal with it?

13) What have you learned from your mistakes?

WILL Type Questions

1) What are your long-range and short-range goals and objectives?

2) When and why did you establish these, and how are you preparing to achieve them?

3) How do you plan to achieve your career goals?

4) What motivates you to put forth your greatest effort?

5) What do you think it takes to be successful in an employment situation like ours?

6) What contributions can you make to our operation?

7) What two or three accomplishments have given you the most satisfaction?Why?

8) Are you willing to spend at least six months as a trainee?

FIT Type Questions

1) What rewards do you expect in your career?

2) What do you expect to be earning in five years?

3) Why did you choose this career?

4) Which is more important to you: money or type of job?

5) How would you describe yourself?

6) How do you think a friend or professor would describe you?

7) How do you determine or evaluate success?

8) What qualities should a successful manager possess?

9) If you were hiring someone for this position, what qualities would you look for,

10) In what kind of work environment are you comfortable?

11) How do you work under pressure?

12) In what part-time or summer jobs have you been most interested? Why?

13) How would you describe the ideal job for you following graduation?

14) Why did you decide to seek a position with us?

15) What do you know about our company?

16) What two or three things are most important to you in your job?

17) What size company are you looking for? Why?

18) What criteria are you using to evaluate the employer for whom you hope to work?

19) Are you willing to travel?

20) Why do you think you might like to live in the community in which our office is located?

Some interviewers ask just one question to begin with, and then immediately throw the ball to the job seeker, like:

"What is your understanding of our meeting today?"

How is that for turning the interview topsy-turvy? But you can tell more from candidates by the quality of the questions asked than by the quality of their answers. The next instruction is even more interesting:

"I would now like you to ask me seven questions."

You can give the candidate permission to ask you any questions at all. No limits. And then you listen. You learn a lot more about people by allowing them to tell you what they think you want to know.

"How would you do this....?"

For interviewers these are powerful and effective questions.

These questions make the candidate tell you how they would approach, handle, deal with, solve, etc., a particular situation, problem, project or challenge that is relevant to the job role in question. The situation could be from his past experience, a hypothetical scenario, or a real situation from the interviewing organisation.

As the interviewer, you should judge the answers objectively. Avoid the temptation to project your own style and feelings into the assessment of whether the answer is good or bad. Look for thoughtfulness, structure, cause and effect rationale, pragmatism. The candidate may not approach the question like you do, but they may have a perfectly effective style and approach to the answer just the same. The answers may indicate their approach, methodology, experience and competency in relation to the scenario to how they get things done, and also the style by which they do it.

The following type of questions will tell you if the candidate is detail-oriented:

1) Have the jobs you held in the past required little attention, moderate attention, or a great deal of attention to detail? Give me an example of a situation that illustrates this requirement.

2) Do you like to work with the 'big picture' or the 'details' of a situation? Give me an example of an experience that illustrates your preference.

3) Tell me about a situation where attention to detail was either important or unimportant in accomplishing an assigned task.

4) Describe a situation where you had the option to leave the details to others or you could take care of them yourself.

The following type of questions will tell you if a person is self-motivated:

1) Tell me about a time when you went out of your way to complete an assignment.

2) Give me an example of a time when a project really excited you.

3) Describe a time when you were unmotivated to get a job done.

4) Tell me about a time when you did more than was expected of you.

5) Tell me about a time when you were given an assignment that was distasteful or unpleasant.

When you use the telephone interview, remember to:

1) fill in missing information on the candidate's resume.

2) question him to determine his level of interest.

3) get a feeling for his communication skills.

4) ask some questions to get a sense of his technical qualifications.

5) decide whether to invite him for a personal interview.

If you are unsure of how to ask the right questions during an interview, you can start by reviewing or writing the job description. Identify the key duties and responsibilities. Then decide what skills are needed to perform these key duties and responsibilities. Finally, draft some open-ended interview questions that will make it necessary for the candidates to explain how they have actually applied these skills in the past.

It is generally good to have 12 to 20 experience-based questions that lasts from 45 minutes to one and a half hours. However, the number of questions you ask is based on the number of distinct skills that you are looking for. For each interviewer on your team, you should prepare at least two questions per skill that the interviewer is responsible for assessing. Also don't give any two interviewers the same questions to ask. The idea is to get as much data from a candidate as you can without giving him an opportunity to rehearse.

It would be beneficial to have structured interviews, that is, interviews where the questions have been developed based on a well done job-skills analysis. This is the best way to ensure that your interviews will be complete, consistent and fair. Also, you will find it much easier to evaluate each candidate's qualifications based on his responses to your questions.

Evaluating the Candidate

Evaluating the candidate is probably the most critical part of the interview, from your standpoint. It is this phase that determines if an additional visit is warranted in the case of a screening interview, or if an offer should be extended. It is crucial that your time be well spent.

The purpose of the evaluation is to get the candidate to talk about himself, and to reveal facts which can be used as predictors of future performance and job satisfaction.

Questions should be avoided when no predictions can be related to the answer. Example of this type may include: "Tell me about yourself" and "Where do you want to be in ten years?" while these questions may get the candidate talking. I have never heard an interviewer explain what constitutes a right or wrong answer.

The questions asked should be open-ended ones, which typically begin with 'why', 'what', or 'who', and should be related to some experience in the candidate's past. A question like, "What did you like the least about your previous job?" clearly has some right and wrong answers for a career in public accounting. If the candidate disliked the pressure of the job, dealing with people, or working long hours, you can be sure he would not be happy with a public accounting firm during the busy season.

What is the value, if any of questions like, "If you were an animal in the zoo, what animal would you be?" Zero value. These questions only satisfy an interviewer's need for an ego gratification. The biggest problem with a question like this is that it has no 'face validity'. The candidate has no idea how to answer such a question, and these questions smack of amateur psychology. So stick to open-ended questions that require a candidate to describe specific job-related events that reflect on their skills.

The next technique you should consider is the restatement. Psychologists believe that when we are asked a question, two answers immediately come to mind: (1) the truth, and (2) what we think the interviewer wants to hear. Most times the candidate give you answer number 2. A restatement will often break through this barrier and get to the truth. A request for restatement lets the candidate know that you are really listening and want to know more. The technique consists of using the candidate's last answer by feeding it back as another question. This is one of the most effective techniques any interviewer has, but it takes practice on your part for it to become conversational. Almost every open-ended question should be followed by a restatement in order to gain greater insight into his personality, likes and dislikes.

At times you have to probe thoughtfully about techniques to get more detailed information about a candidate's response to a question. The process requires that you first ask the candidate to describe a specific job-related experience, like, "Tell me about a time when you had to deal with a disagreeable person". In order to get complete information you will need to ask the candidate to tell you such details as. Who was involved? Where did the event take place? What led up to this situation ? What actions were taken by all parties? What was the final outcome?

Another item in an interviewer's bag of tricks is silence. We have all been in situations where a teacher will ask for an answer, and it quickly becomes obvious to everyone but the teacher that no one has the answer. The teacher starts at the class awaiting the answer, and the pressure builds. The pressure is even greater in a one-to-one interview session where you ask a question and simply stare when the candidate responds. He may, on rare occasions, tell everything he knows, and even make up things. There are few times when this technique is warranted.

How not to ask Questions

Never be very vague when you ask a question. While it is good to sound relaxed and chatty while interviewing the candidate, don't allow the relaxation to make you lose control of the interview. Very rarely will you get a satisfactory response to a question as vague and undirected as, "Why don't you tell me a little about yourself?" The candidate will either say too much or too little, and may later repent for it.

Avoid asking double questions. For example, "Why do you want to join our firm, and where do you see yourself in five year's time? "This type of question can easily confuse or fluster a candidate. So, ask one question at a time.

Avoid asking leading questions which suggest that you have strong opinions, and expect certain answers. For example, "Our main competitor produces adulterated food products. Do you agree?" or "You quit your previous job soon after joining that firm. They are believed to indulge in underhand dealings. Didn't that suit you?" Questions like these are unfair and difficult to answer, and the candidate may feel obliged to answer the way you want. This will definitely jeopardise the atmosphere of mutual trust that you have been trying to establish.

Wait patiently for the candidate to finish answering your question. Do not proceed too quickly to the next question. If his answer is not clear or is incomplete, it will surely leave a bad impression. He may have simply paused to rethink or phrase a sentence. If you are not sure of his answer, you can try to rephrase the answer by saying, "So what you are saying is..." or "In other words..." This will give him the chance to clarify anything that sounds vague, or correct any misunderstandings.

Do not put words into a candidate's mouth. You can certainly step in when you see him floundering for words, and thus rescue him from becoming jittery. But be sure that you don't do it often. Your job is to just guide and control the interview, not to dominate it.

8

Common Problems for
the Interviewer

The adage "Practice makes a man perfect' applies to interviewers also. It takes a lot of experience and skills at interviewing, and only practice can help you achieve perfection. But there are some recognised techniques for handling certain common difficulties.

A Very Nervous Candidate

When you welcome a candidate who looks visibly very nervous, try to put him at ease by extending the welcoming period. Make light and friendly conversation, and make an effort to find areas of common interest with him. His application form will provide you information that will guide you to appropriate topics. A smiling and relaxed attitude on your part will help him to unwind gradually.

Gregarious or Flustered Candidate

When you find that a candidate talks too much, or starts to lapse into long silences, reduce your eye contact. You can interrupt by saying, "Can we move on to..?"or "I would like to talk about..." Ask him one or more closed questions, like, "Did you complete you driving course?" or "Did you attend the French classes recently?" to alter the rhythm of the discussion, forcing him to give only brief, pointed answers.

Very Quiet Candidate

You might encounter a candidate who likes to answer only in monosyllables, and it is very difficult to elicit long answers from him. In such a case, slow down the pace of the questions. Allow reasonable pauses, and coax him to fill these pauses in his own time. Maintain eye contact at all time, and show that you are interested in his replies. Ask open questions, thereby forcing him to give more detailed and expansive answers.

Candidate Seeking Advice

While you show a friendly nature while interviewing, let it not lead to the candidate becoming so familiar with you as to start seeking advice. Don't allow him to start pouring out his personal or professional problems, for then you are in danger of becoming a counsellor rather than an interviewer. Try to steer him quickly back on track directly.

While you show the candidate that you understand his problems, do not get involved in them. Offer only some general and non-partisan advice, and nothing beyond that. As soon as possible, assert yourself and quickly introduce the questions that you want answered. Ask closed questions to which he can give positive, rational answers. This will help in setting an appropriate atmosphere once again.

9
Concluding the Interview

After you have finished with asking your questions, at the end of the evaluation phase, you should indicate that it is the candidate's turn to ask questions. You can use the questions as a way of describing what makes your firm unique, and stressing areas of excellence. You should avoid discussing negative aspects of other firms. Negative comments are unprofessional and probably counterproductive.

The candidate may ask you a particularly astute question, or a particularly stupid one, and this might affect your assessment of the candidate. You can revert the question back to the candidate with a comment like this:

"That's an interesting question! What are your own views on the subject?"

Explain the follow-up procedures after saying a few words about the job or the company. But be sure not to unnecessarily raise the candidate's hopes.

In the last phase of the interview you should try to give the candidate some idea of the decision process, and an estimate of the timing—when a decision will be taken, and when he will learn the results.

At the end of the interview, it pays to give the candidates an indication of their performance. It is also a good idea to ask for their impression of how the interview went.

Then thank the candidate for attending. Never make the mistake of making anyone feel that the interview has been a waste of time. Finally accompany him to the door.

Complete an interview assessment form at once. You will be making notes throughout the interview, but it is essential to make your detailed assessment and evaluation immediately on completion. This will help you make your final decision, especially if you have interviewed many people for the position. Counter your prejudices and preconceptions.

Take a second look at your first impressions. Train yourself to not prejudge a candidate initially as you may subconsciously spend the rest of the interview looking for reasons to back your initial assessment.

Evaluate your own performance while the interview is still fresh in your mind. You can note down:

1) Things you would like to do differently.

2) Ideas you may have for other interviews.

3) Any further questions of the candidate.

4) Questions for a second stage in the interview process.

5) Clarify any scratching, ensure pages are numbered, fill out notes that don't make sense.

6) Write down any observations made during the interview, for example, where did the interview occur, and when; was the candidate nervous at any time? Were there any surprises during the interview?

Give yourself a break of 10-15 minutes to make notes about the candidate while it is still fresh in your mind. The small break also helps to clear your head for the interview of the next candidate.

Come to a definite decision about the candidate as soon as the interview is over, while your impressions are still fresh. You can grade him according to the method you have chosen to evaluate each candidate. Be sure that you don't allow any bias or preference to colour your decision while awarding points to the candidates.

PART - II
The Interviewee

10

Preparing for the Interview

Congratulations! You have been called for an interview. Your moment of truth has arrived. Successful interviewing will be essential in order for you to lock in an offer, and make the most of. To be successful, you should always seek to retain control of the process, and the only way to do it is to have control over the final decision. You can always walk away from a company that you later decide you have no interest in, but you need to remain in positive control to retain the power to pick and choose.

Your objective in every interview should be to take yourself one step further toward generating the job offer. You can do that by doing your very best in each and every interview. Treat every interview as if it were the only one you will ever get with that company, and your only opportunity to convince them that you are the right candidate for the position. Although there may be several interviews before the eventual offer, you must score positively in each interview.

As Norman Vincent Peale says, "Any fact facing us is not as important as our attitude toward it, for that determines our success or failure." Make the most of this achievement by preparing thoroughly for the interview. Careful preparation will give you confidence, control, and the ability to deal effectively with any question you may be asked. That is the theory, so start putting it into practice!

For many first-timers especially, the time before an interview is a tension-filled, nerve-racking period. It would help you if you learn to relax and adopt a positive attitude. The underlying strategy for success is to value yourself.

Although there is an overwhelming evidence to show that interviews are a very inaccurate predictor of successful performance in a job, yet getting a job invariably involves an interview at some stage. So firstly, it may help to look at the interview through the employer's eyes.

The first interview is designed to allow the interviewer to test out whether you measure up adequately to the demands of the job and to assess you against other applicants. The selector will look more closely at evidence which you have supplied in your written application and explore your background in greater depth.

Broadly, the interview is likely to focus on:

1) Your intellectual qualities.

2) What sort of person you are.

3) How realistically you have assessed the job.

4) How closely your skills and abilities match the criteria of the job specification.

There is generally no secret about the list of selection criteria an employer will be looking for. Specifics may vary but all employers will be interested in your enthusiasm and commitment to the job, and how you demonstrate it. Certain core skills will be very relevant to the selection process, such as:

1) Effective communication—Can you express yourself clearly in speech and on paper?

2) Successful team-working—How well do you establish working relationships with others?

3) Managing people—Can you organise others and set

objectives?

4) Analytical and conceptual skills—Can you understand the wider picture and see the implication of decision by assessing facts and data accurately?

5) Time management—Can you plan you work, set priorities and achieve objectives effectively?

It is important that you assess your strengths—examine your weaknesses too, and think about what you can do to improve the situation. No employer expects superhuman qualities! A willingness to train and learn new skills is always important. The interviewers will, however, expect that you have analysed which are the core skills in the job for which you are applying. They will explore these areas in depth within the interview, so prepare well.

Remember, preparation for the interview is as important as the interview itself. By preparing fully you can ensure that you will be calm and collected on your way to the interview, and during the interview you are ready for any questions that are asked.

A job offer—this is your number one goal, and it cannot be stressed enough. You are not interviewing to evaluate the company or broaden your knowledge of available opportunities. You are interviewing to see if you are good enough to get a job offer. An undecided or tentative attitude has no place in a job interview.

You could be just the right candidate for a particular job, but a sloppy, one-size-fit-all job application could spoil it all for you. Make sure you create a good first impression with the application. Once that hurdle is over, and you are called for an interview, make sure that you are well prepared.

The following tips will help you to prepare well for the interview:

1. Research about the Company

Do some research about the company—their size, products, annual sales revenue, principal lines of business and locations, etc. Check their website. This will not only make you feel more comfortable during the interview, but it will also prepare you to show genuine interest in the company.

It is very important to create a good impression. It is always advisable to go to the company's website, and do a little research on the company, their requirements, their potential and so on. Armed with such information, you impress the interviewer even before you attend the interview.

If you are using an employment agency, get the full details of the role, the company, location of the interview, who will be conducting the interview or your contact when you arrive, and also information about the type of interview that will take place.

If you have gone direct to a company, most of the information you need will have been sent to you via a letter. It is suggested that you phone to confirm that you have received it, and that you will be attending the interview. During the phone call you can always ask about the type of interview, if this has not been mentioned in the letter.

A little preparation before the interview will help take the edge off of the event, by knowing as much as possible about the company or organisation you are interviewing with , you will be able to speak about topics that are relevant to the job you are applying for.

You can also research about the company by obtaining brochures, know their financial background, clients of the company. Good places to research information include:

1) The business section of your public library

2) Business and financial magazines

3) Business sections of newspapers

4) your prospective employer's company literature

5) the company's website

6) Online research sources

7) The company's in-house magazines or newsletters.

Learn all you can about the company or organisation. Learn as much as you can so that your questions are sophisticated and knowledgeable during the interview. Employers expect you to arrive knowing background information about the organisation. If you don't you will look like you are not really interested in the job. You have to be able to answer the critical question of why you would like to work for that employer - and not sound like you would accept any job. Research helps you formulate intelligent and appropriate questions to ask in your interview. Be prepared to answer and ask questions.

Research should always be the first step to effective interviewing. Gathering background information on employers is a crucial element in successful interview preparation. You will need to be prepared to answer questions like, "What do you know about our company?" and "Why do you want to work here?" Knowing as much as possible about the company's past performance and future plans can make your interview more interactive, and could be just the leg up you need in a competitive job market. Before the interview, review the company's website thoroughly, and don't be afraid to contract your prospective employer to request details on the position you are interviewing for, or to ask for the company's literature. Researching the company helps narrow down your job search to those that match your needs. At the same time it gives you all the ammunition you need to take on the interview panel.

2. *Learning about Your Interviewer*

If you can learn a little about the person who will be interviewing you, you will be miles ahead of the game. Try to research up one or two things about his accomplishments, history with the organisation, outside interests—anything that helps you break the ice and speak to him about the things he is interested in.

For help in how to get the inside scoop on your interviewer, ask people in your professional and personal network what they know about him. Conduct a research on the internet using the person's name and company name. Read the company's annual report to learn about the company's directions and goals, including those that might involve the interviewer's department. Once you have got some information about the interviewer, compile it in profile.

3. Travel Arrangements

Prepare your travel arrangements, especially if the location of the interview is in an area unknown to you. Make a test trip to establish the best route there the day before you interview. This is very important if your are travelling a long distance by car, or you are using public transport. Leave for the interview at a time to ensure you arrive half an hour before the interview. This will allow for delays, and enable you to be calm and prepared before your interview.

4. Listing Questions to Ask

Make a list of questions that you would like to ask. This may include ones about the company, the role, location of where you would work, plans that the company may have in the future and any others that are relevant. This will show an interest on your part, and that you have prepared well.

The last question you may be asked could be, "What can I answer for you?" Have questions of your own ready to ask. You are not simply trying to get this job, you are also interviewing the employer to assess whether this company and the position are a good fit for you.

5. Practice makes Perfect

Practice with friend, and record your responses so that you

can replay the interview and see how well you did. Prepare answers to commonly asked interview questions. Doing so will help you analyse your background and qualifications for the position.

Commonly asked Interview Questions

While the types of questions differ, depending on the interviewing style, you must plan and be prepared for the typical types of questions. You should not memorise answers, but script specific responses so that you will be able to remember more details when asked the questions in the interview.

As a candidate, you should be equipped to answer the questions thoroughly. Obviously you can prepare better for this type of interview if you know which skills the employer has predetermined to be necessary for the job you seek. Knowing what kinds of questions might be asked will help you prepare an effective selection of examples.

Every confident job hunter would like to think that 'winging it' during an interview is the best policy, perhaps the most natural. However, taking the time to formulate your answers, and solidify your thoughts will give you more poise and security during the actual interview.

The following are some questions that you will have to answer in most interviews. These are standard questions most frequently used.

1) Tell me about yourself.

2) What do you want to do with your life?

3) Do you have any actual work experience?

4) How would you describe your ideal job?

5) Why did you choose this career?

6) When did you decide on this career?

7) What goals do you have in your career?

8) How do you plan to achieve these goals?

9) How do you evaluate success?

10) Describe a situation in which you were successful.

11) What do you think it takes to be successful in this career?

12) What accomplishments have given you the most satisfaction in your life?

13) If you had to live your life over again what would you change?

14) Would you rather work with information or with people?

15) Are you a team player?

16) What motivates you?

17) Why should I hire you over the others?

18) Are you a goal-oriented person?

19) Tell me about some of your recent goals, and what you did to achieve them.

20) What are your short-term goals?

21) What is your long-range objective?

22) What do you see yourself doing five years from now?

23) Where do you want to be ten years from now?

24) Do you handle conflict well?

25) Have you ever had a conflict with a boss or professor? How did you resolve it?

26) What major problem have you had to deal with recently?

27) Do you handle pressure well?

28) What is your greatest strength?

29) What is your greatest weakness?

30) If I were to ask one of your professors or employers to describe you, what would he say?

31) Why did you choose to attend your college?

32) What changes would you make at your college?

33) Has your education prepared you for your career?

34) What were your favourite classes? Why?

35) Do you enjoy doing independent research?

36) Who were your favourite professors? Why?

37) Do you have plans for further education?

38) How much training do you think you will need to become a productive employee?

39) What qualities do you feel a successful manager should have?

40) What made you interested in our oragnisation?

41) What do you know about our company?

42) Do you have any location preferences?

43) How familiar are you with the community that we are located in?

44) Will you relocate? In the future?

45) Are you willing to travel? How much?

46) Is money important to you?

47) How much money do you need to make to be happy?

48) What kind of salary are you looking for?

49) Why did you leave the previous company?

50) Do you feel you are overqualified for the available opening?

Don't just read these questions. Practise and rehearse these answers.

Knowing what kinds of questions might be asked will help you prepare an effective selection of examples.

Use examples from internships, classes and school projects, activities, team participation, community service, hobbies and work experience—anything really—as example of your past behaviour. In addition, you may use examples of special accomplishments, whether personal or professional, such as scoring the winning goal, being elected president of your social service organisation, winning a prize for your article in a magazine, hitting a ton on debut in a test match, or raising money for charity. Wherever possible quantify your results. Numbers always impress employers. Remember that many behavioural questions try to get at how you responded to negative situations. You will need to have examples of negative experiences ready, but try to choose negative experiences that you made the best of or better yet, those that had positive outcomes.

Here is a good way to prepare for behaviour-based interviews. Identify six to eight examples from your past experience where you demonstrated top behaviours and skills that employers typically seek. Think in terms of examples that will exploit your top selling points.

Half your examples should be totally positive such as accomplishment or meeting goals. The other half should be situations that started out negatively but either ended positively or you made the best of the outcome.

Vary your examples; don't take them all from just one area of your life. Use fairly recent examples. Try to describe examples in story form and STAR (Situation-Task-Action-Result).

Behaviour-based interviewing is becoming more common. It is based on the premise that your past performance is the best predictor of future performance. Rather than the typical interview questions on your background and experience, you will need to be prepared to provide detailed responses, including specific examples of your work experience.

The best way to prepare is to think of examples when you have successfully used the skills you have acquired. Take the time to compile a list of responses to both types of questions and to itemise your skills, values and interest as well as your strengths and weaknesses. Emphasise what you can do to benefit the company rather than just what you are interested in.

Almost all of us have questions we would rather not be asked. To avoid going into an interview with anxiety about the possibility of those questions emerging, do two things:

1) Review your resume before you send it out to be sure it does not highlight anything that would instigate conversation about one of your 'dark' issues.

2) Make a list of the questions you are afraid of and practise how you will answer them in a positive way.

Prepare your answers for the type of questions you will be asked, especially, be able to say why you want the job, what your strengths are, how you would do the job, what your best achievements are and so on.

Assemble hard evidence (make sure it is clear and concise) of how what you have achieved in the past–proof–will put you ahead of those who merely talk about it .

Have at least one other interview lived up, or have a recent job offer, or the possibility of receiving one from a recent job interview and make sure you mention it to the interviewer.

Make sure your resume is up-to-date, looking very good.

The best way to answer a behaviour-based question is to use the STAR (Situation-Task-Action-Result) technique. You need to answer all four elements to score well. Action is the most important because it describes what you did, what steps you took, etc.

As part of your preparation for the interview, write down for each selection criterion some examples of things you have done that would demonstrate that you meet the criterion.

Remember to draw significant events in your life, either achievement that you have had, or important decision that you have had to make.

Be prepared to also talk about selection criteria generally before you go into specific examples.

You can prepare for behaviour-based interviews by:

1) Conducting a thorough self-assessment, analysing the type of questions to which you are applying.

2) Understanding the required competencies.

3) Preparing your relevant examples, even those when results did not turn out as planned.

4) Rehearsing your responses to anticipated questions including those to tricky questions, like "Describe an occasion when you conformed to a policy with which you did not agree."

5) Rehearsing answers to questions that probe for consistency such as, "What did you do then?" or "What were you thinking?" or even "How did you feel?"

6) Remembering your success at work, educational, volunteer activities.

7) Making yourself a memorable candidate and piquing the employer's interest, by mastering the art of storytelling. Use specific and vivid examples to describe your relevant past behaviour.

8) Avoiding generic, hypothetical information in your story. You want to create an image of you at work. Make sure your examples meet the employer's needs.

The most effective way to answer questions in a behaviour-based interview is to use the SAB (situation-action-benefit) formula. With SAB, you describe the situation (S), tell what actions you took that made the difference (A), and explain the benefits or results of those actions (B). For example , study the following SAB:

Situation: We wanted to improve our level of customer services. We needed to identify the root cause of each customer service failure and implement corrective actions which would improve our company's overall customer satisfaction levels.

Action: I proposed two approaches: one, creating a database to capture all the complaints, and two, an internal process insuring that when we did make a mistake, a letter of apology was sent to the customer within 24 hours explaining what we did to correct the situation.

Benefit: We saw improved levels of customer satisfaction right away. We were able to measure the information from the database and set some goals. We experienced a significant decrease in customer service failures from one year to the next.

Is it difficult to conjure up your stories right on the spot during the interview? You bet it is. So start preparing right now by thinking back to your successes.

What activities from your past do you recall with pride? What have you organised? What have you analysed and what problem have you solved? Think about your teamwork experiences and leadership roles, when and how you showed your initiative.

Interviews are always stressful, and the best way to reduce the stress is to be prepared. Take the time to review the standard interview questions you will most likely be asked, such as:

Work History

1) Name of company, position, title and description, as also date of employment.

2) What were your expectations for the job, and to what extent were they met?

3) What were your starting and final levels of compensation?

4) What were your responsibilities?

5) What major challenges and problems did you face?

6) How did you handle them?

7) Which was the most/least rewarding?

8) What was the biggest accomplishment/failure in this position?

9) What was it like working for your employer?

10) What were his strengths and shortcomings?

11) Why are leaving that company?

About Yourself

1) Describe a typical work week.

2) How many hours do you normally work?

3) How would describe the pace at which you work?

4) How do you handle stress and pressure?

5) What motivates you?

6) What do you find are the most difficult decisions to make?

7) If the people who know you were asked why you should be hired, what would they say?

8) Do you prefer to work independently, or on a team?

9) Give some examples of your team work.

10) What type of work environment do you prefer?

11) Describe a difficult work situation/project, and how you overcame it.

12) How do you evaluate success?

The New Job and Company

1) What interests you about this job?

2) What applicable attributes/experience do you have?

3) Why do you think you are best person for this job?

4) What do you know about this company?

5) Why do you want to work for this company?

6) What challenges are you looking for in a position?

7) What can you attribute to this company?

8) Are you willing to travel?

9) Is there anything I have not told you about the job or company that you would like to know?

The Future

1) What are you looking for in your next job?

2) What is important to you in that job?

3) What are your goals for the next five/ten years?

4) How do you plan to achieve these goals?

5) What are your salary requirements–both short term and long term?

The following are other questions for which you need to formulate answers:

1) What are your strengths and weaknesses?

2) If you could have your choice of any job, what would it be? Why?

3) What have you done to improve yourself during the past year?

4) Tell me about your greatest achievement.

5) Tell me about your greatest disappointment.

6) Tell me about the best and worst bosses you have ever had.

7) How do you handle your reaction when you don't get what you want?

8) Give me a couple of examples.

9) How do you handle stress?

10) How do you pull a team together when it seems to be going nowhere?

11) What qualities do you prize the most in those that report directly to you?

12) What type of people do you have the most trouble getting along with in the workplace?

13) How do you handle it?

14) What constructive criticism have you received from employers?

15) Everybody has pet peeves. What are yours?

16) What else do you think I should know about you?

The interviewer will also want to learn about your experience and reasons for seeking a new position. He may ask you the following questions:

1) When did you do leave your last job?

2) Why?

3) How long have you been out of work?

4) At your last job, now much of the work did you perform independently?

5) What did you like most and least about your last job?

6) What are some of the problems you have encountered in your past jobs?

7) How did you solve the problems?

8) Do you prefer working independently or as part of a team?

9) What prevented you from advancing in your former positions?

10) What have you been doing since you left your last job?

To learn about your plans for the future, and your motivation for applying for the job, the interviewer may ask the following questions:

1) Why do you want to work here?

2) What do you expect to experience in this job that you did not experience in your past jobs?

3) How do you feel about evening work?

4) How do you feel about weekend work?

5) What are your feelings about carrying a pager?

6) How do you feel about being on call?

7) Assuming we make you an offer, what do you see as your future here?

8) Why should we hire you?

9) Are you considering other positions at this time?

10) How does this job compare with them?

11) If you feel you have any weakness with regard to this job, what would they be?

12) What is your leadership style? Please give examples of this style in a real situation.

13) How do feel about relocation?

14) What could you contribute to our facility?

15) Why are you applying for a position for which you are obviously overqualified?

16) Why do you believe that you can handle this position?

17) You don't have the necessary experience or background for this position, so why would my organisation benefit from handling you in this role?

18) How soon would you be able to start this position if we offer it to you?

19) What weakness in your work habits do you think you need most to work on?

Eventually money will become an issue. Among the questions that may arise pertaining to compensation are the following:

1) What exactly were you paid at your last job?

2) What is the minimum salary you will accept?

3) What salary range are you wishing to be considered for?

4) What are your financial needs?

There are many open-ended questions that the interviewer may ask you, such as the following:

1) Tell me about a time when you demonstrated initiative.

2) Describe a situation when you have motivated yourself to complete an assignment or task that you did not want to do.

3) Think about a difficult boss, professor or any other person. What made him (or her) difficult? How did you successfully interact with this person?

4) Think about a complex project or assignment that you have been assigned. What approach did you take to complete it?

5) Tell me about the riskiest decision that you have made. What were your considerations in making that particular decision?

6) Can you tell me about an occasion where you needed to work with a group to get a job done? What were the challenges and difficulties, and how did you face them?

7) Describe a situation when you or a group that you were a part of were in danger of missing a deadline. What did you do?

8) Tell me about a time when you worked with a person who did things very differently from you. How did you get the job done? Would you work with that person again if given the choice?

9) Describe your three greatest accomplishments to date.

10) Tell me about a situation when you had to learn something

new in a short time. How did you proceed?

11) Can you tell me about a complex problem that you solved? Describe the process you utilised.

12) Give me an example of a time when you had to make a split second decision.

13) Give me an example of a bad decision that you made, and what you learned from that mistake.

14) Tell me about a time when something you tried to accomplish failed. What did you learn from that failure?

15) Tell me about a time when you missed an obvious solution to a problem. What did you learn from that mistake?

16) Tell me about a challenge that you successfully met.

17) Describe a situation when you had to go above or beyond the call of duty in order to get a job done.

18) Please tell me about one or two unpopular decisions you have made.

19) What were the positive and negative outcomes of those decisions?

20) What leadership positions have you held?

21) Describe your leadership style.

22) What aspects of your leadership style have you changed or deleted once you learned that these aspects were not successfuly?

23) Give me a specific example of a time when you used good judgement and logic in solving a problem.

24) Summarise a situation where you successfully persuaded others to do something or to see your point of view.

25) Tell me about a time when you had to use your presentation skills to influence someone's opinion.

26) Give an example of when your persistence had the biggest payoff.

27) How have you most constructively dealt with disappointment and turned into a learning experience? Please give me a concrete example in your life.

28) Tell me about a time when you had to conform to a policy with which you did not agree.

29) Describe a situation in which you effectively developed a solution to a problem by combining different perspectives or approaches.

30) Describe a time when you were faced with a stressful situation that demonstrated your coping skills.

31) Please discuss an important written document you were required to complete.

32) Tell me about a recent situation in which you had to deal with a very upset customer or co-worker.

33) Describe a time when you anticipated potential problems and developed preventive measures.

34) Please tell me about a time when you had to fire a friend.

35) Describe a time when you set your sights too high (or too low).

36) Give me a specific example of a time when you used good judgement and logic in solving a problem.

37) Give me an example of a time when you set a goal and were able to meet or achieve it.

38) What is your typical way of dealing with conflict? Give me an example.

39) Tell me about a time you were able to successfully deal with another person even when that individual may not have personally liked you (or vice versa).

40) Tell me about a difficult decision you have made in the last year.

41) Tell me about a time when you delegated a project effectively.

42) Give me an example of a time when you used your fact-finding skills to solve a problem.

43) Tell me about a time when you were forced to make an unpopular decision.

Your Strengths and Weaknesses

As you prepare for your interview, consider your strengths and weaknesses. Also consider where you demonstrated leadership, solved a problem, increased company profits, made a good or poor decision, handled changing events, handled criticism, met or missed a deadline, and worked as a team. Add to this your knowledge and experience necessary for success in the position. Formulate questions that focus on each competency method. What kind of person are the recruiters looking for?

Mission and value-driven individual

1) What is important to you?

2) What gives you the greatest satisfaction? Tell us something you have accomplished that you are most proud of.

3) What motivates you?

4) What are the values you hold most dear?

5) Are you comfortable sharing your beliefs?

An individual who takes initiatives

1) How do you set goals for yourself?

2) What would do you do during your first 30 days in this position?

3) How did you prepare for this interview?

4) What is it that attracts you to this position?

Doer or administrator

1) What do you enjoy most about what you do now?

2) Describe your typical day.

3) How much of your time do you spend outside the office in a typical week?

4) How do you schedule your time?

An individual who will form close relationship with board members and donors

1) What do you enjoy most about what you do?

2) How do others describe you?

3) How do you make decisions?

4) Do you prefer to be tactful or truthful?

5) What do you think motivates people to volunteer their time? What gives them satisfaction?

A person with an optimistic, can/do attitude

1) What energises you?

2) How do you respond when you experience setbacks or disappointments?

3) How do you go about tackling challenged or overcoming obstacles?

A person able to work within the structure of a organisation

1) What kind of environment do you enjoy working in?

2) What kind of working relationships do you prefer?

A professional with experience and the desire to seek major gifts

1) Tell me about one of your major gift donors.

2) Describe how you secured a major gift from that individual.

3) How do you go about seeking major gifts for this organisation?

A person who is confident

1) How do you prefer being recognised for your achievements?

2) What are your expectations of this position?

3) What personal qualities are utilised in your work?

Although there is overwhelming evidence to show that interviews are a very inaccurate predictor of successful performance in a job, nevertheless getting a job invariably involves an interview at some stage. So firstly, it may help to look at the interview through the employer's eyes.

The first interview is designed to allow the recruiter to test out whether you measure up adequately to the demands of the job, and to assess you against other applicants. The selector will look more closely at evidence which you have applied in your written application and explore your background in greater depth.

Broadly, the interview is likely to focus on:

1) Your intellectual qualities.

2) What sort of a person you are.

3) How realistically you have assessed the job.

4) How closely your skills and abilities match the criteria of the job specification.

There is generally no secret about the list of selection criteria an employer will be looking for. Specifics may vary but all employers will be interested in your enthusiasm and commitment to the job and how you demonstrate it. Certain core skills will be very relevant to the selection process, such as:

1) *Effective communication* – can you express yourself clearly in speech and on paper?

2) *Successful team working* – how well do you establish working relationships with others

3) *Managing people* – can you organise others and set objectives?

4) *Analytical and conceptual skills* – can you understand the wider picture and see the implication of decisions by assessing facts and data accurately ?

5) *Time management* – can you plan your work, set priorities and achieve objectives effectively ?

It is important that you assess your strengths, examine your weakneses too, and think about what you can do to improve the situation. No employer expects superhuman qualities! A willingness to train and learn new skills is always important. The recruiter will, however, expect that you have analysed, which are the core skills in the job for which you are applying. They will explore these areas in depth within the interview, so prepare well.

Preparation of References

As an interviewee, it is good to prepare your reference in advance, and give the interviewer a list of your references with names, positions, employer's details, and all possible contact details. Try to identify referees who will be happy to give you a positive reference, and in doing so, who will support your personality, skills, performance and job history claims.

Provide as many referees as you need to cover the important aspects of your performance and employment history, plus any specific critical requirements of the new job, like accreditation, record, training, vetting, etc.

A healthy list of referees would normally be between three and five people. It seems a lot, but it is more impressive than just a couple. It shows you have thought about it beforehand, and it builds in a bit of leeway for when people cannot be contacted, or fail to respond quickly for any reason.

Generally the more senior and credible your referees, the better. It is perfectly acceptable to list one or two referees from your private life rather than work, especially if you have a job or status that carrier important responsibility.

If you know that particularly significant and favourable referee might be difficult to contact, ask them to provide you with a 'To whom it may concern' open reference letter as to your character and history, signed by them on letterhead–and preferably use and keep hold of the original copy–ask the interviewer to take a photocopy and return the original to you.

Telephone Interviews

"All of the darkness of the world cannot put out the light of one small candle,". Anonymous

Many people do not think of phone interviewing as interviewing. "It wasn't an interview, it was just a phone call." It was still an interview and it could affect your potential career with an employer. So treat it with all the respect due a full interview.

A small number of organisations currently conduct telephone interviews as the first stage of selection. These can range from a basic check to see whether you match the selection criteria to a very probing interview.

There are three basic steps of telephone interviews:

1) You initiate a call to the Hiring Manager and he is interested in your background. The call from that point forward is an interview.

2) A company calls you based upon a previous contact, or after receiving your resume. You will likely be unprepared for the call but it is still an interview.

3) You have a pre-set time with a company representative or manager to speak further on the phone—also an interview.

Most interviewees find the process disconcerting because the usual visual clues are missing, so it is difficult to assess how you are doing. Try to relax and act as you would in a face-to-face interview. Be as enthusiastic as possible, because the interviewer only has your voice to go on, and remember, a smile can be 'heard' down the line!

Don't be afraid to pick up the phone! The telephone interview is by far becoming more and more popular. Many job hunters still get that adrenaline rush even with the phone interviews. But following the tips and/will advice given below with help you master the phone interview, and get you to the next step—the face-to-face interview.

Often, the first step in the hiring process is the telephone interview. Companies and recruiters they employ use the telephone interview to develop a pool of candidates to look at closer, and to pare down the number of applicants for a job opening.

The advantages to the company are:

1) The cost is less.

2) The list of questions can be standardised.

3) The interview can be delegated to a lower level employee.

4) It can be done quickly.

The aims on both sides of the telephone are limited. The caller wants a selection of qualified candidates, and the process screens out many candidates. If the call is a straightforward screening call, the caller will must likely ask about your experience, availability and salary requirements. Your strategy is to provide facts that support your resume, with some context about your performance. Try using numbers and facts to be effective. However, you don't want to volunteer anything that could disqualify you. Make every effort to sound professional but not personal, as this call is not to establish rapport. Since you are unlikely to win the job from a telephone interview your goal is to secure an in person interview with the person who has the authority to hire. Approach the call with that attitude.

Try to reschedule surprise interviews. Say that you have a conflict and suggest a time you can call back. When you call back, be prepared for the call just as you would for a full dress rehearsal.

Have ready at hand:

1) pen, paper, a calculator,

2) the job ad, the resume, the cover letter which you send in response to the ad,

3) a list of your accomplishments which relate to the job you are discussing,

4) research that you have done on the company,

5) a short list of questions about the job,

6) your calendar.

Good preparation is essential. It will result in a good performance, which will enable you to do your best. So work carefully through the following steps.

What have you to offer? Look back through your application form and think about how you wish to project this information at the interview. Remember that the application, for which you burnt the midnight oil to perfect, now sets the agenda for the interviews.

Think about your skills. What evidence will you use in the interview to convince the interviewer that your claims to be a good organiser, an analytical thinker, a successful member of a team and a clear communicator, or whatever it may be, are valid? You need to prepare as many examples as possible, using actual events in your life where you have displayed these qualities. It is important to link experiences in your academic life to other activities, whether in voluntary work, a job, or social activities.

It could be, for example, that the research needed to complete a project demanded extensive thought and initiative on your part to discover valuable information, which you then had to edit into a report format.

Prepare a brief word-picture, which you can use in the interview, that outlines the circumstances, the action you took, and the results you obtained. This example could be used to support your claim to be able to think creatively and analytically, to organise your time effectively, and work successfully to achieve an objective. It might be helpful to remember the STAR (situation-target-action-result) approach – set the Situation, explain the Target, comment on the Action you took, and highlight the *result* you achieved.

Master the techniques of a professional:

1) Smile — comes through in your voice.
2) Speak directly into the phone.
3) Don't smoke, chew gum, eat or drink anything.
   It all telegraphs to your listener.
4) Stand up. Your voice sounds stronger.
5) Avoid 'ah', 'er', 'hum'. This habit is especially noticeable on the phone. This takes practice. So practise.

For a winning performance, observe the following rules:

1) Confirm the caller's telephone number.
2) Be aware that the caller can't see you—can't see your hand gestures, can't see you taking notes.
3) Pace the call. Let the caller do most of the talking, without interruptions.

4) Do use the technique of repeating or re-phrasing questions. It tells the caller that you listened carefully, and gives you time to think about your answer.

5) Avoid the simple 'yes' or 'no' ; add selling points at every opportunity.

6) If you need time to think say so–as in radio, a silence during a telephone conversation is dead air time.

Compensation issues come at the end of the interviewing cycle, never at the telephone stage. You can truthfully say you don't know enough about the job to state a salary figure. And of course, you would need a personal interview to really talk with the company — which is another way to go for the personal interview. Re-affirm your qualifications, express your interest in the job and the company. Say you would appreciate the oportunity to talk about the job further—in person.

Here is a quick tip list for excelling at a telephone interview:

1) Treat the telephone interview as you would a face-to-face interview.

2) Select a quiet private room with a telephone in good working condition.

3) Conduct a mock telephone interview with a friend to gain feedback on your voice quality and speech.

4) Before the interview, prepare talking points for the call including value you bring to the company, and specific questions.

5) Arrange the following items: your "resume", covering letter, copy of application if you submitted one, highlights of corporate information and brief talking point.

6) Breathe deeply and relax, speak slowly, clearly and with purpose.

7) Smile — it changes your speech, and the person on the other end can sense it.

8) Write down the full name and title of the caller.

9) Take notes when appropriate.

10) Be courteous, and try not to speak over the interviewer. If you do, apologise and let the interviewer continue.

11) Support your statements with detailed examples of accomplishments when possible. It is easy for someone to get distracted on a phone call; so point a vivid picture to keep the interviewer interested.

12) Explain any pauses in your speech to ponder a question or take notes.

13) If you think of a question or comment while the interviewer is speaking, jot a note on your talking points list so that you remember it later.

14) During the interview, if the interviewer inadvertently answers a question from your prepared list, cross it off. If you forget and ask it, it will seem as if you were not listening.

15) Offer to provide additional information or answer other questions.

16) Use your talking points list of specific skills and accomplishments. Cross them off as you work them into the conversation. At the end , if you have some uncrossed items, you might say something like , " I thought you might be interested to know I led a major conversion project, quite similar to what you are planning. I managed a Rs. 2.5 crore budget, and completed it 45 days early, saving over Rs. 46,000."

17) Before ending the call, be sure you know the next step in the process, and offer to provide any additional information needed.

18) Do not hang up until the interviewer has hung up.

19) Promptly send a formal follow-up thank-you letter, just as you would for a face-to-face interview.

❖ ❖ ❖ ❖ ❖

11

Before the Interview

The day before the interview, sleep early so that you are fresh and alert during the interview.

Get clear direction to the interview site, and arrive early for your meeting. Unless otherwise instructed (e.g., to fill out a job application), arrive 10 to 15 minutes early for the interview. This shows that you are eager and punctual. If you are not at least five minutes early for an interview, you are five minutes late! But don't arrive half an hour early, as it might be inconvenient for your interviewers and the receptionist. Definitely don't be late! Late arrival for a job interview is never excusable. If you are running late, do phone the company. It would be even better to take a practice run to the location where you are having the interview a day before, or be sure you know exactly where it is and how long it takes to get there. A last minute rush means you will arrive flustered.

Do greet the receptionist or assistant with courtesy and respect. This is where you make your first impression. If you strike up a conversation with another interviewee, ensure you talk softly, and don't disturb around you. If presented with a job application, do fill it out neatly, completely, and accurately. Treat all people you encounter with professionalism and kindness. Remember that the receptionist or assistant or maintenance may offer his or her opinion of you to the boss. This will count, as it also creates a good impression with potential colleagues.

If you feel nervous, try to relax. If you feel the need for support, arrange to have an encouraging friend to accompany you and chat to you beforehand. If the secretary or assistant is not busy, strike up a conversation with her or him. This may help you to relax.

You can also think about what you will do once the interview is over. Whatever the outcome of the interview, you may want to go shopping, see a movie, spend time with a friend-anything that helps you to relax.

Before you speak at the interview, you will be seen. The style of dress you choose depends on the company and the position you are applying for. Your appearance should indicate that you have a grasp of what is acceptable dress within the company. So dress appropriately. Plan how you will dress for the interview.

If you are in doubt about how to dress, you could stand outside the company building at the start or close of business, and watch the employees trooping out or entering, and within 15 minutes you will have a good idea of the range of dress styles acceptable to the management.

Make sure your outfit is comfortable to wear, and that it suits you. You want to make a good impression, but you do not want to distract the interviewer with an overpowering costume.

It is better to use formal dress rather than jeans for an interview. Clothes have to be clean and ironed to represent order and discipline. A professional-looking outfit is bound to impress most employers, even if you would not usually dress up that much every day on the job. A general rule of thumb is to dress one notch above what you would wear on a typical day at work. It shows professionalism and respect, and most important, that you know how to dress for interviews.

For men, a conservative two-piece business suit in solid dark blue or grey is best. You can have conservative long sleeved shirt–white is best, pastel is next best. Wear a solid or striped tie. Ensure that your shoes are clean, polished and conservative. You should have well-groomed hairstyle, and clean, trimmed fingernails, wear minimal cologne. Empty your pockets of tinkling coins.

While a party or a college campus may be perfect forum in which to exhibit your flair for the latest in fashion style, the interview is not the place to do so. With very unusual exceptions, sandals and sweatshirts are out, while business suits are still in. You may not like a necktie any better than the next person, but it is still a fact of life in interviewing. Even though many companies have relaxed the internal dress code, interviews still follow the conservative standard. Don't buck the trend.

Unfortunately, most college graduates who are first-time job seekers are woefully unprepared with proper interview dress. They feel they can get by with what is already in their wardrobe—usually not. Dress for the world outside college is quite different from the campus scene. Remember that stylish is not conservative. You should be doing the talking, not your clothes.

This is not to say that you need to go out and buy a whole new wardrobe. Go for quality over quantity. One or two well-chosen business suits , or a couple of decent pants and shirts, will serve you all the way to the first day on the job and beyond. Then, when you are making some money (and have a chance to see what the standard uniform is for the company), you can begin to round out your wardrobe. For now, no one will fault you for wearing the same sharp outfit each time you interview. If you desire some variety within a limited budget, you might consider varying your shirt/tie/accessories as a simple way to change your look without breaking your wallet.

One final note on interview dress: while it goes without saying that your interview clothes should be neat and clean, very few candidates give the same time and attention to their shoes. Shoes? Yes, shoes! An example is that of a corporate recruiter who forms first impressions based solely on shoes. This person does not have a shoe fetish; he subjectively judges that those who pay attention to details, like their shoes, are also likely to be diligent in their work life. And it is not just that person's opinion. Many have said that you can judge a person by his shoes. You will find that many ex-military officers (many of whom have found their way into management positions in corporate houses) are especially aware of a person's shoes. It is not enough to be clean, pressed, and ironed. Make sure your shoes are conservative, clean and polished.

For women, a well-starched and ironed cotton sari with a matching blouse would be ideal. Those not comfortable in sari, could wear salwar-kameez, or pants and decent tops. Wear shoes, sandals or slippers that are clean, and comfortable. Carry a light purse, nothing huge and garish. If you wear nail polish, use clear or a conservative colour—let the colour not be distractive. Minimal use of make-up, which is not too noticeable, is recommended. keep a positive frame of mind. Set other concerns aside and focus on what you are going to accomplish at the interview. Relax.

When you pack your bag for the interview, be sure to put in a few copies of your resume, a pen, notepad, and that l8ist of questions you want to ask. Also bring samples of your work, if you have any (such as a brochure you wrote or a design you created, or your article which appeared in a newspaper or magazine) that is relevant to the job you are applying for.

Work out, what you are going to wear, in advance. Appropriateness is probably the key word here. It is important that you look smart, but equally important that you are comfortable. Wearing a new suit for the first time after three years in jeans isn't easy. Also make sure that your jewellery is to the minimum. Avoid wearing bright clothes; instead wear clothes that are light-coloured, unless it is a suit. Before entering the interview room, check that your appearance is fine.

Collect and neatly arrange your important papers and samples in a nice briefcase or portfolio. This makes you look organised and professional.

Just as a picture speaks a thousand words, so does a sample brochure, photograph or technical prototype. If you have samples that demonstrate you relevant skills, bring those samples to the interview in a briefcase or small bag. When an appropriate question is asked, refer to your samples as a way of showing your talent. The act of showing the interviewer something tangible will change the pace of the interview, and make a memorable impression about your achievements. By the way, don't bring a sample if it is larger than what you can carry in one hand or more elaborate than what can be taken out of its case and presented in ten seconds or less. Your portfolio should make you look good, not clumsy.

Make sure you take with you the letter inviting you to the interview, and that you know the name of the interviewer (if given).

A copy of your application or curriculum vitae will also be useful. If you are required to take anything else to the interview, have them ready to take to the interview site. Have extra copies of job reference lists, a notepad for taking notes, and any other information that you may wish to have with you. Don't rely on your application or resume to do the selling for you. No matter how qualified you are for the position, you will need to sell yourself to the interviewer. If you have letters of recommendation, don't forget to include them. Bring at least one pen and pencil.

Turn off your cell phone, pager and other devices that might interrupt your interview. Also keep a list of questions that you would like to ask the interviewer when your turn comes.

Avoid carrying documents in an envelope as it will take time to show them to the interviewer. Carry only relevant documents. Certificates of qualifying examinations are important documents. Carrying them in a plastic cover or plastic bag will not give an impression of quality and class. Do not present any certificate or document unless asked for. Remember to collect all the certificates given for perusal at the interview.

Get into a positive thinking mood:

1) I am very good at ...

2) I was successful in ...

3) I was very pleased with my achievement in ....

Remember, an enthusiastic, alert, positive mindset will take you far.

12

During the Interview

If you get the jitters when you go for a job interview, you need these tips. With the following practical and strategic tips, you will sail through a winning interview.

When you are in a good interview, it is like being on a relay team. You and the employer are runners on the same team, and you both have a common goal to figure out if you and the employer's organisation are a winning combination. So think of your interview as a sports event where you and the interviewer pass a 'baton' back and forth. One good question leads to a good answer, which leads to another good question.

Before you know it, 30 or 40 minutes have gone by. You have both learned a lot about each other, and made your selling points. Using this image of cooperation rather than one of opposition will help you have an effective interview. Of course, not all interviews are going to be that fluid. Some interviewers are not skilled at asking good questions. Some may even try to try you up with tricky questions. The interview is the final step of the hiring process, and the most important. This is where you get to exchange information, so that the interviewer and the interviewee find out if their needs match. First you have to answer the interviewer's questions and then you have time to put your questions across and clarify any doubts that may be present in your mind. This process of answering and asking questions will not be difficult if you are prepared.

Do phone ahead, if you are running late for an interview, as soon as you can, and apologise to your interviewer when you arrive. Remember, your interview starts the minute you walk in through the door and lasts until you exit from that door. So, keep your best foot forward from start to finish.

A useful tip is to think through the opening moments of an interview. Make sure you get off to an excellent start with a confident smile and a firm handshake. Remember that first impressions count. There is nothing like a confident handshake. The right amount of tension in your grip is important—not too tight, not too limp. If you are greeting him with a 'namaste' be sure to bend your head slightly, keeping your palms together, and a bright smile on your face. Eye contact is actually a form of communication and it has a magical ability to build a good rapport. So make eye contact with your interviewer, both when you are talking and when he is talking.

During the interview try to remain as calm as possible. Try to have a good posture that shows you are alert and focused. Avoid negative body language. In other words, don't cross your arms over your chest, don't clinch your fists, don't clutch your purse or briefcase tightly, or do anything that might indicate insecurity, hostility or resistance to change.

Try to answer all questions as well as you can. Always be clear while answering. If you do not know the answer to a questions, or if you forget it at that moment, just tell the truth straight away than answering with 'yes' or 'no' or trying to elicit the answers from memory at that moment. Ask for clarification if you are not sure what has been asked and remember that it is perfectly acceptable to take a moment or two to frame your responses, so you can be sure to fully answer the question.

Follow the interviewer's leads, but try to get him to describe the position and the duties to you early in the interview process. This way, you may be able to apply your background skills and accomplishments to the position.

Establish a good rapport with the interviewer. People want to hire those they feel most comfortable with.

In the interview your response needs to be specific and detailed. Candidates who tell the interviewer about particular situations that relate to each question will be far more effective and successful than those who respond in general terms.

Ideally you should briefly describe the situation, what specific action you took to have an effect on the situation, and the positive result or outcome. It is difficult to prepare for a behaviour-based interview because of the huge number and variety of possible behavioural questions you might be asked. The best way to prepare is to arm yourself with a small, arsenal of example stories that can be adapted to many behavioural questions.

Make sure that your good points come across to the interviewer in a factual, sincere manner. Stress your achievements, for example, sales records, processes developed, saving achieved, systems installed, etc.

Respond to questions being asked as they relate to the position, or the company's needs. If asked about your background, be specific, and only talk about those aspects that relate to the particular position in question.

If you get the impression that the interview is not going well, and that you have already been rejected, do not let your discouragement show. Once in a while an interviewer who is genuinely interested in you may seem to discourage you as a way of testing your reaction.

A great way to build rapport with the interviewer is to use his name when you answer a question. So learn his name and if it is a tricky one, practise the pronunciation beforehand so that it will roll off your tongue during the interview.

During the interview, the interviewer will try to evaluate your skills, capabilities, and levels of experience. When as a prospective employee you find yourself sitting in the hot seat, keep in mind that, while there are no standard responses, your replies should be clear and relevant. Stopping in silence to gather your thoughts is not only helpful but wise.

Always offer positive information, and avoid negativity at all times. Get directly to the point. Ask if the interviewer would like you to go into great detail before you do. Discuss only the facts needed to respond to the question. Focus and refocus attention on your successes. Remember, the goal is not to have the right answers so much as it is to convince the interviewer that you are the right person.

Be truthful, but try not to offer unsolicited information. Try not to open yourself to areas of questioning that could pose difficulties for you.

Listen carefully to everything that the interviewer says, and answer with an appropriate balance of confidence and modesty. Respond with answers based on PAR (Problem, Action, Result). What was the problem you faced? What action did you take to solve it? What was the result?

Shift your interview from an interrogation to a dialogue by occasionally finishing your answers with a relevant leading question.

Be prepared to tell stories that demonstrate how you work with people, as the interviewer is undoubtedly curious as to how you will fit in with his staff. Remember to weave your stories into the answers of pertinent questions.

Avoid discussing salary at the first interview. If pressed, respond with something like, "I would seriously consider any reasonable offer you care to make." If it is your final interview, delay talking about salary history and expectations until you fully understand what is entailed in the job, and you have had time to think about what is fair.

When introduced to potential co-workers, be friendly. Your interviewer may be watching to see how you interact with his staff, and may later ask them how they liked you.

Make sure you talk about why you are interested in this position, and what you can offer the company.

In a nutshell, the following points need to be remembered:

1) Knock at the door, and then enter, even if your name is called out.
2) Greet the interviewer(s) as soon as you enter.
3) Sit down only after you are asked to.
4) Remember to say "Thank you" before being seated.
5) Avoid pulling a chair. Instead, lift it if necessary, and always enter from the right side of the chair.
6) Sit without crossing legs, and sit straight.
7) Look at the interviewers instead of looking down.
8) Keep whatever paper materials you carry on you lap, and not on the floor.
9) Bend forward while answering questions.
10) While answering a questioner, remember to look at the other interviewers also.
11) Avoid fidgeting, like touching your moustache or your hair, scratching your nose, etc.
12) Avoid carrying anything like a key bunch or a pen in your hand.
13) At the end of the interview, get up and move out only after thanking the interviewers.
14) While moving out, step back first, then turn and walk away.

Always make sure that your body language is sufficiently receptive and positive. Be sure that you don't walk in with a chewing gum in your mouth!

❖   ❖   ❖   ❖   ❖

13

The Interviewee's Behaviour

Attire, body language and manners count during interviews. After all, interviewers are regular people like the rest of us, easily impressed by good behaviour, and just as easily offended by inappropriate behaviour.

Interviews can be very formal and structured. Most of the questions will be formulated to uncover your past behavioural patterns, and will be rather rapid in pace. On the other hand, they can be informal and conversational, such that if the pieces of your background will be uncovered in a more random way. Let the interviewer set the tone, and match your style with theirs, in accordance with your individual personality. Although there is not one way of interviewing, there are standard steps that apply to every interview process.

First of all, dress appropriately. Plan how you will dress for the interview. Remember that there is only one chance to make a good first impression.

Keep a positive frame of mind. Set other concerns aside, and focus on what you are going to accomplish at the interview. Relax.

When you walk in, do greet the interviewers by title (Dr. Mr. Mrs.) and last name if you are sure of the pronunciation. If you are not sure, do ask the receptionist about the pronunciation before going into the interview.

Smile. Immediately offer a handshake, introduce yourself, and say something like, "I'm pleased to meet you."

Or

"I've been looking forward to talking with you."

Be sincere and avoid informal greetings you might use to say hell to friends. Take the polite, conservative route. Do shake hands firmly. Don't have a limp or clammy handshake!

Do wait until you are offered a chair before sitting, and then thank them before sitting. This shows good manners. And do remember body language and posture. Sit upright, and look alert and interested at all times. Don't fidget or slouch.

When you are being interviewed, it is very important that you give out the right signals. You should always look attentive, so do not slouch in your chair.

The interviewer has probably decided in advance where you should sit. But if you have a choice, don't sit in a low, soft armchair. It invites a submissive, slouching position in which you cannot easily control your body language. If the chair has arms, avoid putting your elbows on them. This suggests a tense, unattractive posture. By sitting upright, with your back firmly supported by the chair, you will create a better impression.

Always be aware of your body language. An 'open' posture, with your back straight, and arms and legs uncrossed is better than a closed posture where your back is hunched, and your arms and legs are tightly crossed.

Sit with good posture. If you don't know what to do with your hands, keep them clasped on your lap. This is another indication of good manners. Avoid small fidgety movements. However calm your facial expression may be, you will give away your nervous feelings, and distract the interviewer if you keep waggling your foot, smoothing your hair, or biting your fingernails.

If it is possible without making a commotion, scoot your chair a little closer to the interviewer's desk, or take the chair close to the desk, like you are ready to dive in. This shows interest and confidence, but don't invade the interviewer's personal space.

Read the mood. If the interview is formal, then you probably should be too. If the interview is casual, then follow along, while remaining courteous and professional. In either case, try to appear to be relaxed, but not too relaxed. It is not a good idea to put your feet up on his desk!

Interviewers make allowances for nervousness, but try to avoid obvious fidgeting signs.

Maintain eye contact with the interviewer. Avoid staring, or you might make him uncomfortable, but don't look away too often either. To some, failure to maintain a comfortable level of eye contact indicates that you are lying, reaching for answers, or lacking confidence. Keep looking at the interviewers instead of other things in the room, or out of the window.

Never lie to anyone in an interview. Your body language and tone of voice, or the words you use, will probably give you away. Classic body language giveaways include scratching your nose, and not looking directly at the interviewer while speaking to him.

Don't smoke, even if the interviewer does and offers you a cigarette. And don't smoke beforehand so that you smell like smoke. And do brush your teeth, use mouthwash, or have a breath mint before the interview.

Don't ever interrupt the interviewer, even if you are anxious and enthusiastic about answering the question. Answer questions in simple single sentences. Avoid giving additional information unless asked for. Avoid repeating answers, phrases or words. Use a language that is easy to understand but formal in its usage.

Don't eat, drink, chew gum or smoke, or even ask if it is all right to do so. But if the interviewer offers coffee or other beverages, it is all right to accept. It is probably better to say 'no, thanks' to snacks (unless you are at an interview meal), so that you don't accidentally drop crumbs in you lap, be forced to talk with your mouth full, and all that other stuff your mother told you not to do with food.

If you are attending an interview meal, do follow all good eating manners that you were taught. For example, put your napkin in your lap, don't order anything messy and complicated, avoid bad-breath foods like garlic and onions, chew with your mouth closed, keep you elbows off the table, and order only moderately-priced items from the menu. Don't order booze, even if your interviewer does. Let him pick up the tab, and be sure to thank him for the meal.

While answering questions, do avoid using poor language, slang and pause words like 'uh', 'um', 'er'. Don't be soft-spoken. A forceful voice projects confidence. Don't be shy or self-effacing. You want to be enthusiastic, confident and energetic, but not aggressive, pushy or egoistic. That fine line is important. If you find yourself trying hard to sell yourself, you are probably crossing the line. Instead, pull back, be confident, reassuring and calm.

Interviewing is based on taking turns; the better you are at listening, the better you will know when to speak and what to say. The interviewer has to be aware that you are listening carefully, pause when answering to note his responses. Try to tune in to the interviewer, and show that you recognise who is in charge. So wait for him to finish before you speak. You might get the feeling that you are failing to establish a good rapport with the interviewer. Perhaps, you are at fault. Consider the following:

1) Are you talking too much? Pause more often and shorten your answer.

2) Maybe your answers are so short that they sound curt. Soften your tone, and by means of nods and gestures, show the interviewer that you are interested in the questions and comments.

3) Respond with well thought out answers, speak clearly, and use facial expressions as a visual aid to emphasise your meaning.

Don't make negative comments about previous employers or others. Listen very carefully to each question you are asked, and give thoughtful, to-the-point and honest answers. Ask for clarification if you don't understand a question. It is all right to take a few minutes of silence to gather your thoughts before answering. Try not to beat around the bush or take a ling time to give the answer that the interviewer is seeking.

Do avoid controversial topics. Don't act as tough you would take any job, or are desperate for employment.

Do make sure that your good points come across to the interviewer in a factual, sincere manner. Then don't ever lie. Answer questions truthfully, frankly and succinctly. Whenever a question demands it don't answer with just 'yes' or 'no'. Explain and describe those things about yourself that showcase your talents, skills and determination. Give examples. Do show off the research you have done on the company and industry when responding to questions.

Don't bring up or discuss personal issues or family problems. And make sure you don't joke during the interview. Don't respond to an unexpected question with an extended pause or by saying something like, "Boy, that is a good question!" And do repeat the question out loud or ask for the question to be repeated to give you a little more time to think about an answer. Also, a short pause before responding is acceptable.

Do remember that an interview is also an important time for you to evaluate the interviewer and the company he represents. Do ask intelligent questions about the job, company or industry. Don't avoid asking questions, for it shows lack of interest. Do show what you can do for the company rather than what the company can do for you.

Avoid any disagreement with the interviewer unless it involves your belief systems. If you have to disagree with him do it politely after expressing regret or asking for pardon. Be aware of mannerism, and keep a smiling face so as to welcome any question. If you are complimented for the answers, remember to thank the interviewer. If your answer or opinions are rejected by him, remember to say sorry. It is also unwise to contradict an answer through a subsequent answer. If an error is brought to your notice, accept it gracefully.

Exude confidence but not arrogance. Be firm when you are sure, otherwise start statements with 'I think' or 'As far as I know'. Mouth all words clearly, and speak loud enough to be clear. Don't ever raise your voice even when the question comes in that manner. Remain calm, and don't get provoked.

Your behaviour should convince the interviewer about the quality of personality that you have. Avoid any exhibition of emotion about an answer that you consider very dear or correct. If you are asked about achievements or successes, you should take care to list only those which can be proved with evidence. Give authentic information about any details connected with your biodata. When asked any question, answer immediately without wasting time. Avoid being humorous or ironical in your answers.

It is acceptable to ask questions to better answer the questions the interviewer asks you. But withhold the bulk of questions until he asks if you have any, which is typically toward the end of the interview. Avoid asking the frivolous, just because he expects you to have questions. Instead, ask about important matters, such as job duties, management style and the financial health of the company. It is not good to ask about vacation, sick days, lunch breaks and so on, right off the bat. Ask about the lesser matters of importance during follow-up or second interviews.

Typically you will negotiate salary, benefits, perks and such others in a follow-up interview. Regardless, don't bring it up until asked, yet be ready to discuss it at anytime.

Make sure you understand the employer's next step in the hiring process. When and from whom you should expect to hear next. Know what action you are expected to take next, if any.

Always thank the interviewer for his or her time at the close of the interview and establish a follow-up plan. When the interviewer concludes the interview, offer a firm handshake and make eye contact, then depart gracefully.

Group selection enables the employer's selection panel to observe behaviour and interaction in a group situation. Job promotion candidates in these situations should therefore behave in a way that will impress the selection panel in areas which the employer logically expects the group selection process or exercise to highlight.

Here are the sorts of behaviours that impress when demonstrated by group selection candidates: responsibility, integrity leadership, maturity, enthusiasm, organisation, planning, creativity, noticing and involving quiet members of the group, calmness under pressure, and particularly discovering and using other people's abilities in order for the team to achieve given tasks. For interviewers, the same principles apply in new employer job interviews.

Interviewers commonly assess interviewees according to their own personal style and approach. For example, friendly people like friendly people; results-driven people like results-driven people; dependable reliable passive people like dependable reliable passive people; and detailed correct people like detailed correct people.

14

Taking Questions

"To be a great champion, you must believe that you are the best. If you are not, pretend you are." – *Muhammad Ali*

You are a special person. You know it. Your mom knows it. Your dad knows it. Your siblings know it, but probably won't admit it to anyone else. Your friends and relatives know it. But unless you convince the interviewer of your special talents and abilities, you will fade into that great abyss of 'interviews lost'.

More and more employers are conducting a different type of interview than they did five or ten years ago. Known as "behaviour-based interviews", these interviews are filled with behaviour-based questions designed to elicit patterns of accomplishments relevant to the employer's situation. They are specific and challenge interviewees to provide concrete examples of their achievements in different types of situations. Such interviews are based on the simple belief that how a job candidate has responded to certain types of situations in the past is a good predictor of how that person will behave in a similar future situation.

Behaviour based questions are likely to begin with some variation of:

138

1) Give me an example of a time when you …..

2) Give me an example of how you ….

3) Tell me about how you ….

This is an opportunity for you to sell your positives with an example or two. Briefly describe the situation, enthusiastically explain what you did, and indicate the outcome.

Preparation is the key. Many of the questions are standard, so try to anticipate them. Your answers should match the job requirements to your experience and skill. Avoid using cliches such as," I'm a people person," in defining your qualifications. Instead, use concise, considered and specific examples taken from real experience.

Put yourself in the interviewer's position, listening to the same cliches and pat answers. You should have unique stories that allow the interviewer to remember you. Give examples that are very specific. You have to find a creative way to communicate the fact that fit their job, and have the interviewer remember you.

Rapport is vital to the success of the interview. One method of establishing it is physically altering your behaviour to match the interviewer's behaviour. Match the rate of speech, volume of speech and posture of the person conducting the interview. Establishing rapport helps people communicate on the same plane.

Obviously you want to select examples that promote your skills and have a positive outcome. Even if the interviewer asks about a time when something negative happened, try to select an example where you were able to turn the situation around, and something positive came out of it.

For example, if asked, "Tell me about a time you made a bad decision," try to identify an example where:

1) Even though it was not the best decision, you were able to pull something positive out of the situation.

2) Although it was a poor decision, you learned from it, and in the next similar situation you made a good decision, or know how you will handle it differently the next time a similar situation arises.

3) It was a bad decision but the negative outcome had only a minor impact.

In other words, try to pull something positive–either that you did or you learned–out of even a negative experience you are asked to relate.

Your interview is likely to last from 20 to 30 minutes. During that time the interviewer will try learn the following:

1) The level of your experience and skills

2) Your willingness and ability to learn

3) A sense of your personality, professionalism and commitment

4) An indication of how you would fit into the organisation

5) Answers to specific questions.

Many managers have been trained in giving behaviour-based interviews, so you are likely to run into them. Others will ask traditional questions, in which case, give behaviour-based answers whenever possible. Even when asked traditional questions, take every opportunity to tell a short story about one of your accomplishments, a scenario that demonstrates your style of work, or an example of your skills in action. Your behaviour-based answers will make your interview more memorable, more meaningful and more fun for the manager.

The following are some interview questions that might be asked of you going for a position at any level in an organisation. After each question, you will find an analysis of the question, which may help you understand how to answer such a question in your job interview.

1) *Tell me about yourself?*

Although this question is broad, keep your answer focused and relevant to the job you are applying for. Be precise and concise while answering this question. Mention the top three or four aspects of your experience, skills, interests, and personality that should indirectly substantiate how you will be fit for the job.

2) *What made you interested in our organisation?*

This is the employer's attempt to know whether you know the organisation well. Always be prepared to answer this question. You should have gathered relevant information in advance about the organisation that you have approached for a job.

3) *Why should we hire you over the others?*

The answer can reveal your confidence and goal-orientation. you can explain how your skills are crucial for the opening, and how your high level awareness of the company would easily help you fit into the job and produce wonderful results. Citing instances where you have solved difficult problem in your previous organisation will help here.

4) *What are your long and short-term goals?*

Good question! The interviewer is trying to get a feel for why you want this job, and how long you are going to stick with it. The ideal answer will assure the employer that you are worth his investment, that is, training you, introducing you to clients, entrusting you with responsibility. Your answer should assure him that you will be around for a while–and maybe even a long time.

5) *Outside of work, what are some of the things you do?*

Employers know that what an applicant does for free can speak louder about his character than what he does for money. Tell the interviewer about something in your non-professional life that says, "Hey, I'm a good person!"

6) *What strengths do you bring to this job that other candidates might not?*

There is no hidden message here. The employer is giving you the floor to sell yourself for the job. Prepare well for this answer, and deliver it with confidence. After all, who knows more about why you are suited for the job than you? And make your presentation, using brief achievement stories whenever possible.

7) *What is your major weakness?*

Of course you should be truthful at this point too, but do not be overly negative. Quite often you can turn a weakness into a positive statement. For instance, you can say "I am too involved in my work, and I sometimes work till midnight to see that the job on hand is finished" or "I tend to ask questions until I am clear about an issue."

8) *Do you consider this a lateral or vertical career move?*

This question is designed to find out how challenged you will be on the job. Be careful, it is a double-edged sword. If you are not challenged, you will get bored and move on. If you are too challenged, you might not make it past the first week. Try to come in somewhere in the middle, maybe, say something to the effect of "It's a comfortable stretch". Your answer will also give the employer a sense of whether you are hoping for just a little or a big increase in salary.

9) *Why do you want to leave your current position?*

Well, the interviewer is concerned about any problems that might crop up on your next job, especially since that might matter with him. Be sure to use good judgements here. Badmouthing your current boss is the worst thing you could do in an interview. The interviewer knows that if you say this today the same thing will be said about him at some other place. Don't badmouth your current boss, and don't bring up anything negative. Even if your boss was a Satan, just say you had ideological differences, and after much trial and error, have agreed to disagree. A safe approach is to say something like: "It's time to move on in my career," or "I'm looking for a greater challenge."

10) *Why did you leave your last job?*

Sounds like the interviewer wants to know if there are any underlying problems like: lack of commitment, difficult personality, poor performance, or anything that might lead to termination. Employers don't want to take on someone who has a record of walking out on jobs or getting fired. No matter why you left your last job, couch your response in positive terms, without lying.

11) *Please explain why you have a gap in your employment history.*

With this question, the employer is looking for any problems in your personal life that might become his headache if he hires you. Explain your gaps honestly, leaning on activities that support your job objectives, if that is possible. If you don't have anything to say that is relevant, then talk about activities that show your strength of character, and helped you know what you really want to do next; the job you are interviewing for.

12) *You seem to be overqualified for the available opening.*

This is one among the many reasons given why you are not the person for the job. You can turn this objection into opportunity. "You are correct in saying that I am overqualified for the post, but I think I will start being productive for you that much faster; you will need much less effort to train me." If the objection is that you do not have any work experience, politely reply that you are confident that as long as you have the necessary skills and confidence and willingness to do a good work, you do not think experience actually matters.

13) *Of all the problems you had at your previous position, which was the hardest to deal with?*

What a sneaky question! "Of all the problems..." Don't fall for it. Don't let on that you had lots of problems, even if you did. Instead, refer to an area you—and probably the rest of the world—find challenging, and move right on to how you have learned to deal with it.

14) *What project required you to work under pressure? And what were the results?*

How you respond to this question will tell the interviewer whether or not you like working under pressure. Be honest and positive. All jobs bring with them a certain amount of pressure, but some have a lot more than others. So give an example where the level of pressure was just right for you, which will suggest how much pressure you are looking for on your next job.

15) *What college experience are you especially proud of?*

If you have not been in the workplace long, this question is your opportunity to give balance to the fact that you don't have much paid experience. Spotlight your academic and extra-curricular achievements, especially the ones that are relevant to your job objectives.

16) *What classes or training are you planning to pursue at this point?*

This one is tricky. You want to look dedicated to developing your profession but you don't want to appear to have so much going on that you won't be 100 per cent on the job. Make it clear that your number one priority is your job; developing your profession is second.

17) *Where do you see yourself in the next five years?*

This is a question that can really trouble you. Do not panic. You can say five years seem to be a really long time, and say what position you think you would be occupying in a year's time. You can also say that even though you are sure to put in sincere work, you can't really answer the question till after you have been in the field for some time.

18) *What salary do you expect?*

Answer this one carefully. Try to avoid mentioning a fixed amount at the very first instance. Ask the interviewer, how much would he be willing to pay a person with your qualification, skills and experience. You can say you are well qualified, and you have done a good job in your previous company, and were paid a certain amount.

If you are going for a management position, you may be asked a few questions not asked of non-management folks. These questions may pertain to:

1) Budget
2) Company policy
3) Management style
4) Conflict management
5) Consensus building
6) Team development
7) Organisational systems
8) Supervisory skills
9) Goal achievement
10) Public relations
11) Investor relations.

All cases fall into two broad categories — long and short (the reference being to time). Listen to the interviewer for cues on this issue, and know the structure of the interview before going in. Odds are you will never get started with a long one, and you will find that, more often than not, you can gauge what your interviewer is looking for if he leans forward and says, "Okay," let's start with a quick case to get warmed up." This does not mean, please ramble on for the next 45 minutes, pulling every rabbit out of your pocket. If he throws down his pencil, leans back, rolls up his sleeves, and takes about 10 minutes to formulate the question giving you every fact including names, dates, etc., odds are your answer should be longer than, 'yes', they should expand." It is all a matter of reading his cues both at the start, and while you are answering. As you get more experienced, you will also recognise that certain types of cases are usually long ones, while others are quicker. That comes with experience. The following are the types of cases you will come across.

1) Brain Teasers

"Why are man-hole covers round?"This is a famous brain teaser question, and no one is sure if anyone knows the real reason. The case interview answer, however, is, "So that you can't fall into the man-hole, if someone drops them, for example." You can have other answers as well: "They are heavy," for example, but then you are becoming rather creative, aren't you? It might or might not work. Brain teasers are those little puzzles that your parents used to tell you, and are a fairly popular way to get the interview going (sometimes to wind it down) . Your answer should be quick, relaxed and even include a sense of humour about the whole thing.

Some of the sample brain teasers can be:

a)   You are in the forest on your way to town A. You come to a fork in the road, where the road splits in two, each going to a different town. You know that all the people from town A tell the truth, while all the people from town B lie. There is a person standing there, but you don't know which town he comes from. You have a question—how do you make it to town A?

b) There are eight balls, one of which is slightly heavier than the others. You have a scale that you can use for weighing, but you are only allowed to use it twice. How do you find the heavier ball?

c) You have 18 blue socks and 14 black ones in a drawer. It is very dark. How many do you have to pull out before you have a matching pair?

d) You have 2 empty jugs. One holds 3 gallons, the other holds 5. How do you get exactly 4 gallons of water from the tap?

2) Market Sizing

These are also generally short questions, though your answer should be somewhat longer than for brain teasers, "How many blue washing machines were sold in Delhi last year?" We will save you the suspense — you will never know the right answer, and the interviewer too doesn't know it. What this type of case tests is your ability to structure a problem, make certain assumptions, do rough calculation, and explain your reasoning to the interviewer. The last thing you should do is say , "13,000", or "10,000." A typical explanation follows the lines of "Let's say there are 9 million people in Delhi, with an average household size of 3. That makes 3 million households. Let's say that 50 per cent of them live in houses, 50 per cent of them having their own washing machines. That makes about 1.5 million washing machines in houses. Out of the 1.5 million people living in apartments, let us say 10 per cent have their own washing machines. That makes another 15,000 washing machines in apartments. That makes a total of 1,65,000 machines in Delhi. Let's assume that washing machines break own once every five years and need to be replaced. That means 33,000 new washing machines are sold every year in Delhi.

Let's say that 20 per cent of these are blue. That means 6,600 blue washing machine were sold in Delhi last year.

Before you applaud, let's make it clear—we have no idea how many blue washing machines were sold in Delhi last year, nor do we really care. However we did demonstrate an ability to structure a problem, make reasonable assumptions, and we demonstrated that we are comfortable calculating 20 per cent of 33,000. That is what the interviewer is looking for. You can use a pen and paper to keep track of your figures, and you should always use round numbers (never say 12 per cent — you are shooting yourself in the foot !). Don't get too detailed as you will lose the interviewer, as well as drag the process out far much. Be concise, detailed and organised.

A sample market sizing can be as follows:

a) How many book publishers are there in Delhi?

b) How many students appeared for JIPMER exams in India last year?

c) How many double-decker buses are there in India at present?

d) How many new apartments were built in Bangalore last year?

e) How many HP printers were sold in India last year?

3) Project

Project cases are generally long. They can be written or oral, and involve a typical situation facing a business. Generally, the interviewer will pick an industry with which he thinks you might not be familiar (such as the golf ball manufacturing industry), and ask you to analyse the problem facing the client. The client might be looking to expand into a new product line, a new geographical location, attempting to target a new demographic, facing a rushing cost structure, or any other typical problem that companies face every day. You will be given a minimal amount of information. As you start to structure your problem, you will realise you need other pieces of information. This shows that you understand what issues are relevant, and reveals to the interviewer what types of information you would spend your time gathering. If they don't have the information, they will tell you to make an assumption, and you should do so in the market sizing. The project case is an interactive dialogue between you two, where you should continually be asking questions, and "thinking aloud." The interviewer will often steer you in the direction he thinks you should go, and you should follow his lead. These cases can take anywhere from 15 minutes to an hour. The interesting ones are when the interviewer asks you about a case he has actually worked on in the past, and then tells you what really happened in real life.

Simple project questions could be:

a) You are consulting for a major distillery in Hyderabad. They mainly produce a mid- priced beer and two different brands of mid-priced gin. Every year, their profits are shrinking. What could be causing this?

b) You are consulting for a small manufacturer of motorcycles. They handcraft their bicycles and are well reputed for having some of the best quality on the market. A large multinational competitor has announced that it will begin selling high-end motorcycles incorporating the newest engine technology. What should your client do?

c) You are consulting a major distributor of canned foods in India. They are considering an expansion into the Middle East market. What would you recommend?

d) You are consulting for one of the largest supermarket chains in the country. This chain is considering opening its own bank branches in its supermarket locations. What is your advice?

e) You are consulting for a major airline in India. Every year, they make more sales, and every year they lose more money. What could be causing this?

The following are some questions you might find yourself answering in your executive interview:

1) *Tell me about a time when you developed or reorganised a procedure successfully.*

   Here is your chance to look good by talking about one of your favourite achievements. While telling your story, keep in mind what tasks you might be asked to perform at the job you are applying for, and highlight anything in your story that relates to your next job.

2) *When did you initiate a policy or project and how did your idea affect the company?*

   Employers love to hear how you affected the bottom line, since it implies that you will be able to do the same for them. Tell a story that demonstrates that you understand how success is measured in your line of work, and that you are able to achieve it to the satisfaction of your employer.

3) *Could you describe a challenging problem you solved, and what the long-term of your solution was?*

   Most of us hate to admit that we have problems, but the truth is that we do. It is how we handle problems that shows our real talent. So dig deep and come up with a time when you either took on a problem and solved it, or you were in the middle of a project, and the problem came up unexpectedly.

4) *What was the toughest budget issue you ever faced? Could you tell me about it?*

   Budget management is a big deal to employers. Before you decide how to answer this question, decide how involved you want to be with the budget on your next job. If you want to manage a budget, talk about a time when you did a terrific job with the money. If you hate dealing with budget, tell about a time when you worked with someone else on the budget.

5) *Tell me about a creative approach you used to increase profits.*

There are two ways to increase profits: decrease spending and increase revenue. This question is designed to find out if you are going to bring new profit-making ideas to the company, especially ones that work. So tell about a time when you either cut costs or increased revenues.

6) *Give me an example of how you built consensus within you team.*

An effective manager gains buy-in from his staff so that everyone experiences success, both individually and as a group. To respond to this question, you could speak about one of your experiences in morale building, creative incentive programmer, or using your fine management style to increase cooperation among your staff.

7) *When did you have to resolve conflict among your subordinates?*

Conflict resolution is a valuable skill. With downsizing, mergers and problems in corporate management, this could be your winning ticket. Put yourself in the interviewer's shoes to know what interpersonal issues are current stumbling blocks at the company. Then come up with an experience of your own that parallels the company's.

8) *When have you had to represent the company or your department before a group of people?*

Here is your chance to show where your presentation skills lie. If you love speaking before groups, great. Tell about some winning presentations you have done. If you are not really comfortable in front of large groups, refer to a time when you delivered a message to either a small group or to an individual, and don't forget to emphasise the positive result of your presentation.

9) *When did you have to sell an idea within your company, and how did it work out?*

The employer wants to know how much courage and persuasion you have. Think of a time when you persuaded someone or a group to follow your lead to a successful end. Your experience might have been around a serious business matter, or maybe even a personal interaction that turned into a humorous take.

10) *What skills, experience and training do you have that make you qualified for the job?*

Give examples of professional and outside experiences that relate to the job. Be specific. Many people talk about how they have a lot of energy or commitment. That is really not a skill or experience.

11) *What is your management style?*

There are several commonly accepted management styles, ranging from laissez-faire, which is extremely laid back, to autocratic, when one person makes all the decisions. Avoid the cliché, "It depends on the situation." Scrutinise your own management style. Team- building is characteristic of many organisations today. An integrated management style sees value in team members participating in the decision-making process.

12) *Give me an example of a decision you made that benefited your company.*

Give an example that sets you apart from other candidates. A good example would be a decision that had a positive effect on a lot of people in the organisation. A candidate for a project manager's job could talk about how a creative solution to a problem benefited the organisation either financially or through improved efficiency. If it is important for a candidate to demonstrate leadership or initiative, then give specific examples showing leadership or initiative skills.

13) *What would your boss say about you?*

This is a question that many people don't think about because they don't think it is going to come up. But often bosses are called up for references, additional information or insight into the person's work ethic or background. As an employer, it is important to know whether someone is leaving a company because he has had a positive relationship and simply wants continued professional growth or if other factors are involved. If a candidate is defensive and uptight, the interviewer will immediately suspect there has been a rift; if there has been a conflict, explain it in a positive way. The candidate should show that an effort was made to resolve the conflict. Be up front—explain if there was an organisational structure or different management style that did not allow you to resolve the conflict. Also, bosses can be one of the best recommendations you can ever get.

14) *What is your biggest strength?*

This is another standard question. The strengths should match the most important aspects for the position. If it was an entry level engineering position, perhaps the individual should stress technical expertise. If it is a job for a management position, maybe it is an individual's ability to establish rapport or long-term interpersonal relationships with team members that would be the person's strength. Give two or three examples. Tell how you grew in the firm. Your progressive responsibility, which is one of the buzzwords can be linked to show why that would be valuable to your next employer.

15) *What most or least interests you in the position we have?*

Do your homework and be able to cite things, such as the commitment of the organisation to professional development. Keep it to a major theme like the ability to grow within the organisation and develop professionally. But specifically back it up. What least interests you in the position should be minor in nature. One response is to ask the interviewer for clarification about something that came up during the interview.

When answering behaviour-based questions, do try to steer clear of the pat answers which interviewers are adept at spotting. For example, don't try to portray yourself as a person that never makes mistakes. Or as a person whose only failings are that you work too much, are too dedicated, too loyal, etc. Be honest about your mistakes since the experienced interviewer will be looking for progress and growth, not perfection. But do give an example of how you learned from your mistake, and how that experience has benefited you in the long run.

Be succinct and concise. In all behavioural answers, the interviewer wants to hear:

1) A brief description of the problem, challenge or situation.

2) What your action was, and how you decided that action.

3) A brief description of the result of your action and your assessment of its result.

When dealing with questions that put pressure on you or create stress, be confident, credible and constructive by accentuating the positive in your answers. And make sure you prepare.

Stress and pressure questions come in all sorts of shapes and sizes. Three commonly used types of pressure questions are those dealing with weakness and failure, blame, and evidence of ability or experience.

Weakness and Failure Questions

"Tell me about your failures…"

"What are your greatest weaknesses?"

These are the interviewer's equivalent to:

"Are you still heating your wife?" Don't be intimidated by these questions. You don't have to state a failing or a weakness just because the interviewer invites you to.

"I don't really fail," or "I really can't think of any," are perfectly acceptable answer. Short and sweet, and then wait, smiling for the comeback. You will have demonstrated that you are no mug and no pushover. If you are pressed (as you probably will be), here is your justification answer, or if you wish to appear a little more self-effacing use this as a first response, "I almost always succeed because I plan and manage accordingly. If something is not going right I will change it until it works. The important thing is to put the necessary checks and contingencies in place that enable me to see if things are not going to plan, and to make changes when and if necessary." Or, "There are some things I am not so good at, but I would never say these are weaknesses as such—a weakness is a vulnerability, and I don't consider myself vulnerable. If there is something I cannot do or don't know, then I find someone who can do it or does know. "Do you see the positive orientation?" Turn it around into a positive every time.

Blame Questions

Watch out also for the invitation to rubbish your past job or manager, especially in the form of, "Why did you leave your last job?" or "Why have you changed so many jobs?"

The interviewer is not only satisfying his curiosity, if you say your last boss was an idiot, or all your jobs have been worthless, you will be seen as someone who blames others and fails to take responsibility for your own actions and decisions.

Employers want to employ people who take responsibility, have initiative and come up with answers, not problems. They do not want to employ people who blame others. So always express positive reasons and answers when given an opportunity to express the negative. Never blame anyone or anything else.

A great technique for exploiting the blame question trap is to praise your past managers and employers. Generosity is a positive trait, So demonstrate it. Keep your praise and observations credible, realistic and relevant. Try to mention attributes that your interviewer and prospective new employer will identify and agree with. This will build an association and commonality between you and the interviewer, which is normally vital for successful interview outcomes. They need to see that you think like they do, that you will fit it.

You can turn questions like, "Why have you changed so many jobs?" into positive ones by saying, "I was ready for more challenge," or "Each job offered a better opportunity which I took," or "I grow and learn quickly, and I look for new opportunities," or "I wanted to get different experiences as quickly as I could before looking for a serious career situation, which is why I am here."

Prove-it Questions

These can be the toughest of the lot. Good interviewers will press you for evidence if you make a claim. So the answer is, be prepared. Watch out for closed questions, such as, "Can you do so and so....?" "Have you had any experience in...?" These questions invite a 'yes' or 'no' answer, and will be about a specific area. If you answer 'yes', be prepared to deal with the sucker punch, "Can you give me an example?"

The request for example or evidence will stop you in your tracks if you are not prepared or cannot back up your answer. The trick is before the interview to clearly understand the requirements of the job you are interviewed for. Ask to see the job description, including local parameters if applicable and any other details that explain the extent and nature of the role. Think about how you can cover each evidence that is qualified and relates to commercial or financial outputs.

Companies are interested in people who understand the motion of maximising return on investment, or return on effort. If your examples and evidence stand up as a good cost-effective practice, they will clock up even more points for you. Make sure you prepare examples of the relevant capabilities or experience required, so that you are ready for the 'prove-it' questions. You can even take papers or evidence material with you to show. Having hard evidence, and the fact that you have thought to prepare it, greatly impresses interviewers. If you don't have the evidence, then don't bluff it and say 'yes' when you would be better off saying, "no, however...". Use "no, however..." and then your solution or suggestion, if asked for something that you simply don't have. Give an example of where previously you have taken on responsibility without previous experience, or full capability, and made a success, by virtue of using other people's expertise, or fast-tracking your own development or knowledge or ability.

On this point, good preparation should include researching your employer's business, their markets and their competitors. This will help you relate your own experience to theirs, and will show that you have bothered to do research yourself.

In summary, to deal with pressure questions, keep control, take time to think for yourself, don't be intimidated or led anywhere that you don't want to go. Express every answer in positive terms.

Competency-based Questions

These questions commonly start with a scenario and a question as to how you would deal with it. Or the question might ask you to give an example of how you handled a particular challenge or situation in the past. He might ask how you would approach a current situation in their own organisation.

In these cases, the interviewer will often judge your answers according to how much he agrees with your behavioural approach. The questions may initially seem or be positioned as competency-based, but often he will be treating this really as question of behaviour and style.

Without going to unreasonable lengths, your answers should reflect the style expected/preferred/practised by the interviewer or the company.

Handling Like-minded Interviewers

Interviewers often have a weakness for people who are like them. For instance, a result-driven interviewer, certain high-achieving dominant personalities, aspiring managing directors, certain ruthless types will warm to answers with a high results-based orientation. It could be an answer like, "I focus on what needs to be done, to cut through the red tape and peripherals, ignoring the distractions," etc.

Alternatively, if you find yourself being interviewed by a persuasive, friendly, influential, egocentric types, then frame your answers to mirror that style: "I use persuasion, inspiration, leading by example, helping, providing justification, reasons, empahasising with the situation and people who are doing the job, motivating according to what works with different people, understanding what makes them tick."

Human Resource interviewers are often 'people-types' and will warm to answers that are sensitive, and take strong account of people's feelings, happiness, well-being, sense of fairness and ethics, honesty, integrity, process, accuracy, finishing what has been started, having a proper plan, steady, reliable, dependable, etc. —the language of the fair and the disciplined.

Technical interviewers, for example, managing directors who have come up through science, technical, finance disciplines, will warm to answers which demonstrate the use of accuracy, plans, monitoring, clearly stated and understood aims, methods, details, checking, measuring, reporting and analysing.

These are all generalisations, of course, but generally relevant in most interview situations when you are asked, "How would you....?" Obviously, be true to yourself where you can. It is a matter of tint and orientation, not changing your colour altogether.

Occasionally you might meet a really good interviewer who is truly objective, in which case mirroring is not so useful, whereas confidence, maturity, integrity, flexibility, compassion, tolerance, pragmatism are, and as such should be demonstrated in the way you answer questions of a balanced mature non-judgemental interviews.

Interviews can be a bit of a game, so when you see that it is, play it. The more you see subjective judgement and single-track behaviour in the interviewer, the more advantage there is in mirroring the interviewer's style in your answers.

As an interviewee, be aware that even the most objective interviewer—even if aided by psychometric job profiles and applicant test results—will always tend to be more attracted to applicants who are like them, rather than applicants who are unlike them. It is human nature.

When you attend promotion interviews as a candidate, your answers should be orientated to match the style preferences of the interviewer. Try to see things in the way they see them, and express your answers and ideas in a language and terms that they will relate to and understand. Don't distort the truth or make claims you cannot substantiate or deliver. Show that you understand how your boss and/or the interviewer sees the situation, and how they see that the job needs to be done successfully.

Over-qualification Problems

Candidates searching for jobs, especially those with solid experience and varied backgrounds, sometimes hear, "I'm sorry, but you are overqualified" is frustrating, but it does not always mean you are out of the running. It means you have to understand, and then allay the fears of the hiring manager, and face the issue head-on in your interview.

Defuse the issue. Employers believe that as soon as the company picks up, you will leave, and they will have to start all over with a candidate search and the new employee training curve. The best way to avert the concern is to be the first one to broach about it at the interview. Your goal is to defuse their objections with a carefully crafted pitch on how your qualifications will pay off for the company. Then be honest about your reasons for a lower level position.

It is all right to say, "I have worked at a higher level, but I want to earn a living and this job and duties appeal to me." Don't say, "I can't find anything else out there." Strongly state your commitment to stay a minimum amount of time to give you both a chance to try each other out.

It is all acceptable to say, "I would like to learn this industry, and I am willing to take a lower-level position to do that." Or, "I have been on the bench for over a year. I have kept myself active and learning but I do like to contribute. I am not looking to fill time. I am looking for a job with long-term employment possibilities."

If you have other reasons, such as changed family or

personal circumstances that have led you to apply for the
position, be honest about them.

The Issue of Salary

A related issue is a candidate's salary expectations. Many
employers don't believe a candidate will take a lower-level job
and the accompanying salary, and cut the interview process
short for efficiency's sake. To prevent this from happening,
indicate that you are flexible on salary during your initial
discussion. Don't mention how much you used to make.
Research the appropriate salary range for the position you are
applying, and make sure the employer knows you are willing
to take that salary level.

15

Tackling Tricky Questions

While most interview questions are generally straightforward, unambiguous inquiries, some interviewers will throw in surprises specifically intended to explore your thinking and expectations at a deeper level. Or they may be meant to throw you off guard to see how you react in high stress or confusing circumstances. Or they may not be intentionally tricky at all. They may merely be invented by the interviewer, or borrowed from lists of questions available on the internet, with no idea what their value is, or how to assess your response as it relates to the requirements of the job.

How you answer tricky questions could determine whether you would receive an offer from the organisation. But it is also important to remember that what those questions are, and how your answers are received, can tell you volumes about whether this is a company you want to work for. Here are some of the questions you might want to consider as you are preparing yourself for a job interview:

1) What aspects of your career you feel especially good about, and how you can make sure those are discussed in the interview.

2) What aspects of your career so far you feel especially worried about discussing.

3) How you can formulate answers to questions about these aspects in advance.

4) How you can use the interview to learn about the potential interviewer.

Tricky questions make a candidate uncomfortable for any number of reasons. They are too personal; they are not obviously related to the open position; they require fast thinking under hypothetical circumstances, or they prompt the candidate to reveal crucial information, such as salary expectations, before he is ready to do so.

If the question is subtle or complicated, don't be ashamed to ask the interviewer to repeat it. Think about it what you have been asked, and try to order your thoughts before you answer.

Don't allow yourself to be overwhelmed. Don't undersell yourself by giving up on a difficult question without first trying to answer it.

Some questions, especially questions in which you are given a scenario and asked to think your way through to a solution are designed to help the interviewer understand your ability to make tough decisions, or be a leader in high pressure situations. True, it is reasonable to expect that you will not ever find yourself stranded in a lifeboat, charged with deciding which fellow survivor to throw overboard to conserve rations. But the way you reason out your decision may tell the interviewer much about you, for example, how you would choose which product to take out of inventory to conserve valuable warehouse space. Try to answer these kinds of questions based on business strategy.

Do keep your sentences short and to the point. Once you have completed your answer, indicate to the interviewer that you have finished what you wanted to say. One way to do this is to drop the pitch of your voice on the last syllable of your final sentence.

Some questions ask you to divulge your greatest weakness. Such questions are usually designed to discover the extent of your self-knowledge. We all have weaknesses, and it is unreasonable to expect you to be perfect in every way. Keep your answer short and dignified. Identify only one area of weakness that you are aware of, but also describe what you are doing to strengthen that area. Don't try to be too clever by turning a negative into a positive, saying things like, "My biggest weakness is that I am a determined worker, and won't give up until the job is done well and completely," you are not fooling anyone.

Sometimes you get the impression that the interviewer does not know why you are being asked a certain question, and that your answer would be beyond his understanding. How do you salvage the situation? A company that hires unqualified interviewers to select qualified candidates may not be one you would like to work for, so you may want to salvage such a situation. But if you are determined to give yourself the chance to work at this organisation, help the interviewer out by exploring the reasons behind the question and what exactly is being looked for in the way of response. Even though you may not answer the question itself, you will still benefit from the conversation. You will position yourself in the interviewer's mind as someone who is not rattled by ambiguity, but instead works calmly and cooperatively with team members to arrive at the best possible outcome. The interviewer would end up taking it as a positive trait of the candidate in all probability.

Put yourself in the interviewer's shoes, and assume that he is slightly uncomfortable with the process at well. Few people relish meeting someone new, and peppering them with probing questions. So he may feel tired of the same old questions and the same pat rehearsed answers. Remember also that he was once sitting in your seat, applying for his job within the company and worrying about the same surprise questions that you are doing. The resulting empathy will help break down the barriers of tension and perceived judgementalism.

Prepare yourself in advance by identifying the topic areas that might be the trickiest for you. Then think carefully about how you might answer them. Broadly speaking, there are eight areas of questioning that could pose a challenge for you:

1) Your experience and management skills

2) Your opinion about industry or professional trends

3) The reasons why you are leaving your current job

4) Financial or other values of your past achievements

5) Your work habits

6) Your salary expectations

7) Your expectations for the future

8) Your personality and relationship skills or problems.

Imagine which of these might be discussed, and formulate in advance the general thoughts and responses you want to express. But don't rehearse answers to anticipated questions word for word.

Never lie. Interviewers can detect it by your body language as they are trained to do so. They are more experienced at hearing the answers that candidates think they want to hear than you are at delivering them. Be candid and clear, and use lengthy answers only when you see that demonstrating your strategic thought process in detail will add valuable information.

Do end your answers with positive points whenever you can. For instance, if you offer some criticisms of the company that last employed you, try to end your comments with a couple of positive remarks about the company. You want to show that you are not biased, that you are able to make an even-handed assessment of your employers, pros and cons.

When in doubt, try to understand the business reason behind the question.

Fielding Tough Questions

Be prepared to encounter most of the following tough and tricky questions in your interview.

1) *Why do you want to work here?*

   To answer this question, you must have researched the company. You should reply with the company's attributes as you see them. Cap your answer with reference to your belief that this can provide you with a stable and happy work environment—the interviewer's company has that reputation — and that such an atmosphere would encourage your best work.

2) *What kind of experience do you have for this job?*

   This is a perfect opportunity to sell yourself, but before you do, be sure you know what is most critical to the interviewer. He is not just looking for a competent engineer, accountant or salesperson, but someone who can also contribute quickly to the current projects. When interviewing, companies invariably give everyone a broad picture of the job, but the person they will hire will be a problem solver, someone who can contribute to the specific projects in the first six months. Only by asking will you identify the areas of your interviewer's greatest urgency, and therefore interest. If you do not know the projects you will be involved within the first six months, you must ask. Level-headedness and analytical ability are respected, and you will naturally answer the question more appropriately.

3) *What did you like/dislike about your last job?*

   Most interviews start with a preamble by the interview about his company. Pay attention, as this information will help you answer the question. In fact, any statement he makes about the job or company can be used to you advantage. Use this to highlight all the positives of your last job. Criticising a prior employer is a warning flag that you could be a problem employee.

4) *Why are you leaving your present position?*

If your current company is not meeting your expectations, you can often explain this in a positive way: "I need to be challenged to develop my potential further. I am interested in additional responsibility and new opportunity, which unfortunately are limited at my current company because of the company's six/limited product and company restructuring/downsizing. The reputation and market focus of your company offers many opportunities for someone with my training and experience. It is the ideal environment I have been seeking."

5) *How long would you stay with the company?*

The interviewer might be thinking of offering you a job. But employers are aware that the marketplace is such that new hires often do not stay with the company more than two years. Your reply might be, "I would like to settle down with this company. As long as I am growing professionally, there is no reason for me to make a move."

6) *Have you done the best work you are capable of doing?*

Say 'yes' and the interviewer will think you are a has-been. As with these questions personalise your work history and include the essence of this reply! "I'm proud of my professional achievements to date, but I believe the best is yet to come. I am always motivated to give my best efforts, and in any job, there are always opportunities to contribute when one is alert."

7) *How long would it take you to make a contribution to our company?*

Again be sure to qualify the question: in what area does

the interviewer need rapid contributions? You are best advised to answer this question with a question: "That is an excellent question. To help me answer, what do you anticipate my responsibilities will be during the first six or seven months?" Give yourself time to think while he concentrates on images of your working for the company. When your time comes to answer, start with, "Let's say I started on Monday the 17th. It will take me a few weeks to settle down and learn the ropes. I will be earning my keep very quickly, but making a real contribution (hesitant pause). Do you have a special project in mind you will want me to get involved with?" This response could lead directly to a job offer, but if not, you already have the interviewer thinking of you as an employee.

8) *What would you like to be doing five years from now?*

The safest answer contains a desire to be regarded as a true professional and team player. As for promotion, that depends on finding a manager with whom you can grow. Of course, you will ask what opportunities exist within the company before being any more specific. "From what I know and what you have told me about the growth here, it seems operations is where you need the effort, and where I could contribute most toward the company's goals."

9) *What are your biggest accomplishments?*

Keep your answers job-related, and a number of achievements should spring to mind. Do not exaggerate attributions to major projects. You might begin by replying, "Although I feel my biggest accomplishments are ahead of me. I am proud of my involvement with…I made my contribution as part of that team, and learned a lot in the process. We did it with hard work, concentration, and an eye for the bottom line."

10) *Can you work under pressure?*

You might be tempted to give a simple 'yes' or 'no', but don't. It reveals nothing, and you lose the opportunity to sell your skills and value profiles. Actually, this common question comes from an unskilled interviewer, because it is close-ended. As such, it does not give you the chance to elaborate. Whenever you are asked one of these provide a brief yet comprehensive answer, and seize the opportunity to sell yourself. For example, you could say, "Yes, I usually find it stimulating. However, I believe in planning and time management in order to reduce panic deadlines within my area of responsibility."

11) *How much money do you want?*

This is a knockout question: give the wrong answer, and you will immediately be eliminated. It is always a temptation to ask for the moon, knowing you can come down, but that is a poor approach. Companies have strict salary ranges for every job, so giving an ill-considered answer can reduce your job offer chances to zero. Try saying, "I am making Rs.... I'm interested in this opportunity, and I will seriously consider any reasonable offer you care to make me."

12) *What are you looking for in your next job?*

Avoid saying what you want the company to give you. You must say what you can give to your employer. The key word is 'contribution': "My experience in my present job has shown me I have a talent for motivating people. This is demonstrated by my team's absenteeism dropping 20 per cent, turnover steadying at 10 per cent, and production increasing 15 per cent. I am looking for an opportunity to continue that kind of contribution, and a company and supervisor who will help me develop in a professional manner."

13) *Describe a difficult problem you have had to deal with.*

This is a favourite tough question. It is designed to probe your professional profile, especially your analytical skills. You can say, "Well, I always follow a five-step format with a difficult problem. One, I stand back and examine the problem. Two, I recoginse the problem as the symptom of other, perhaps hidden, factors. Three, I make a list of possible solutions to the problem. Four, I weigh both the consequences and the cost of each solution, and determine the best solution. And, five, I go to my boss, outline the problem, make my recommendation, and ask for my supervisor's advice and approval." Then give an example of a problem and your solution.

14) *What would your references say?*

You have nothing to lose by being positive. If you demonstrate how well you and your boss get along, the interviewer does not have to ask what you dislike about your current manager. The higher up the corporate ladder you climb, the more likely it is that references will be checked. It is a good idea to ask paid employers to give you a letter of recommendation. This way you know what is being said, and it reduces the chances the company will have to check references.

Do avoid unnecessary personal disclosures. Certainly there are some matters that you are legally or morally bound to reveal—medical problems, for example, or personal problems that might affect your work. But other private matters may be best kept to yourself, particularly if they have no bearing on the job.

Be careful and avoid using jargon to impress the interviewer. You can use technical or specialised language if you are absolutely sure of its use. Misusing it will make you look foolish. When in doubt use plain English.

When you are asked a tricky question, take time to assemble your thoughts instead of launching into an answer at once. It will impress the interviewer when you think things through in silence, and then provide a well-constructed answer.

Avoid rambling on and on till you are interrupted. If the interviewer keeps interrupting, you are not answering concisely enough.

Avoid playing for time or making comments such as. That's an interesting question !" while nodding your head wisely. If the question is a very difficult one, ask the interviewer if it would be possible to return to that question later. If it is not possible, and you cannot answer the question, say so frankly, instead of hedging.

Always use specific examples instead of talking in the abstract, else this may give the impression that you cannot or will not commit yourself to a firm opinion. Avoid using words such as 'one' or 'people', but be personal with specific examples; "In my experience..", "When I was at...,"I think that ..." and so on.

Be careful that you don't undersell yourself by being apologetic. Don't say, " I have had only four months, experience in this kind of work." This gives the impression to the interviewer that you are under-qualified. If you are unsure of your ground, say so. Avoid long, apologetic introductions such as, "Of course, it is just my opinion, and I may be wrong. But I think perhaps...."

Avoid harping unnecessarily on failures or ill luck. If circumstances forced you to confront something unpleasant in the past, point out the positive side of what at first glance seems negative.

Never make the mistake of exaggerating your current salary in the hope that this inflated figure will be matched or bettered by your prospective employer. An experienced interviewer will probably be able to estimate your income fairly accurately, and will know when you are misleading him.

❖ ❖ ❖ ❖ ❖

16

Questioning the Interviewer

It is now your turn! As the interview comes to a close, a final question that any good interviewer would ask is whether you have any questions to ask. One of the final questions you may be asked is, "What can I answer for you?" This last question is frequently the most important one. Do not think it is rude or pushy to ask a question to the boss. Remember that you are not going to win any humanity contests. Your response at this point often determines if you continue as a job seeker or transform into a job getter. You are not simply trying to get this job, but you are also interviewing the employer to assess whether this company and the position are a food fit for you. The interviewer wants to know whether you are inquisitive and come up with proper questions.

Have interview questions of your own ready to ask. Having no questions prepared sends the message that you have not been thinking about the job. Avoid asking questions that are clearly answered on the employer's website and/or in any literature provided by the employer to you in advance. This would simply reveal that you did not prepare for the interview, and you are wasting the employer's time by asking these questions. It is important to develop intelligent, probing questions of your own that will help you get the information you need to make an informed decision.

Remember that an interview is a two- way conversation. For you, the interview has two purposes: one, to sell yourself, and two, to evaluate the position.

You ask these questions for two reasons. Obviously, the first reason is to get information. Secondly, the interviewer will probably judge you based on the quality of your questions. Remember, the employer should not be the only one asking questions during the interview. After all, you are trying to decide where you want to spend eight or more hours a day for the next few years. Insightful questions help both of you determine if your relationship will be mutually rewarding.

Of course, even great questions will not get you a job offer if you come in with other problems. Here, in order, are the ten attitude strike-outs that most often condemn job candidates:

1) Not asking questions
2) Condemnation of past employer
3) Inability to take criticism
4) Poor personal appearance
5) Indecisiveness, cynicism, laziness
6) Overbearing, over-aggression
7) Late to interview
8) Failure to maintain eye contact with the interview
9) Inability to express clearly
10) Overemphasis on money.

If you don't ask questions in the interview, many employers will wonder if you will avoid asking questions on the job. If an interviewer sets up a scenario for you (a technical candidate) and you do not ask qualifying questions he will wonder if that is how you would approach an application development project. Do no let ego get in the way of asking tough questions.

Employers expect candidates to ask enough questions to form a good opinion about whether they want the job or not. If you, as a candidate, don't ask enough questions, employers who may otherwise be willing to make you an offer may nevertheless reject you because they have no confidence that you know what you would be getting into. At the end of the day they need to feel satisfied that you have enough information on which to make decision in case they make an offer.

Open-ended questions that generate information-rich answers signal to an employer that he is talking to a resourceful candidate who knows how to make informed decisions, a skill vital to any job.

There are so many things you can screw up in a job interview, and not asking thoughtful questions when you have the opportunity is probably the biggest one. All interviewers want to know how candidates collect information. This is a real chance for you to shine and set yourself apart from all the other job seekers.

The questions you ask, and how you frame them, do as much to differentiate you from the competitions as the questions asked by the interviewer. As you prepare for the job interview, your questions have to be as carefully coordinated as your suit and shoes.

Thoughtful questions emphasise that you are taking an active role in the job selection process, not leaving the interviewer to do all the work. Great questions demonstrate that, far from being a passive participant, you are action-oriented and engaged, enforcing your interest in the job.

Asking questions is an excellent way to demonstrate your sophistication and qualifications. The questions you choose indicate your depth of knowledge of your field as well as your general level of intelligence. Asking questions also enables you to break down the formal interviewer's candidate relationship, establish an easy flow of conversation, and build trust and rapport. The matter of rapport is important. Remember, most finalists for a job are more or less evenly matched in terms of qualifications. What gives the winning candidate the nod is rapport.

Your questions steer the interview the way you want it to go. Questions are a form of control. You can also use questions to divert an interviewer's line of questioning.

The more senior the position you are seeking, the more important it is to ask sophisticated and tough questions. Such questions demonstrate your understanding of the subtext and context of this position, as well as your confidence in challenging the interviewer. Hiring managers will judge you as much on the inquiries you make as on the responses you provide. If you don't ask sufficiently detailed questions, it will demonstrate lack of initiative and leadership qualities that a senior-level position demands.

Rules for Framing Better Questions

1) Ask open-ended questions.
2) Keep them short.
3) Don't interrupt.
4) Getting to 'yes'.
5) Use inclusive language.
6) Ask questions that the interviewer can answer.
7) Avoid questions that are obvious or easy to determine.
8) Avoid 'Why' questions.
9) Avoid asking questions that call for a superlative.
10) Avoid leading or loaded questions.
11) Avoid veiled threats.
12) Avoid questions that hint of desperation.

13) Don't ask questions that focus on what the company can do for you.

14) Don't ask questions that are irrelevant to the job or organisation.

15) Never ask about salary and benefit issues.

16) Avoid questions that relate to vacations and retirement.

Great Questions to ask

1) What is the make-up of the team as far as experience is concerned? Am I going to be a mentor or will I be mentored?

2) What does this company value the most, and how do you think my work for you will further these values?

3) What kinds of processes are in place to help me work collaboratively?

4) What is the most important thing I can do to help within the first 90 days of my employment?

5) What would a normal working day be like?

6) Is it possible to move between departments?

7) How much contact is there with management?

8) Is this position more analytical or people-oriented?

9) How soon could I expect to be advanced to the next level in the career path?

10) How much travel is normally expected?

11) Will I be expected to meet certain deadlines?

12) How often are performance reviews given?

13) How much decision-making authority is given after a year?

14) How does the company provide any educational benefits?

15) Have any new product line/services/curricula been announced recently?

16) How would you describe the responsibilities of the position?

17) Is this a new position? If not, what did the previous employee go on to do?

18) What is the company management's style?

19) How much people work in this office/department?

20) Is relocation a possibility?

21) What are the typical work week? Is overtime expected?

22) What are the prospects for growth and advancement?

23) How does one advance in the company?

24) If I am extended a job offer, how soon would you like me to start?

25) When can I expect to hear from you?

26) What is the size of the division, sales volume earnings?

27) Does the company plan to expand?

28) What are the company's strengths and weaknesses compared to its competitors?

29) What are the significant trends in the industry?

30) Could you explain your organisational structure?

31) Can you discuss your take on the company's corporate culture? What are the company's values?

32) How would you characterise the management philosophy of this organisation?

33) Are any acquisitions, divestitures, or proxy fights on the horizon?

34) What do you think is the greatest opportunity facing the organisation in the near future?

35) How will my leadership responsibilities and performance be measured? And by whom and how often?

36) What qualities do you prize the most in those that report directly to you?

37) How does this organisation rank within its field?

38) What is the reputation of the department to which I am applying?

39) How is this department perceived within the organisation?

40) What have been its goals in the last year, and did it meet them?

41) What would be the goals of the department in the coming year?

42) Do you think those are aggressive or conservative goals? Who set them?

43) What problems or difficulties are present in the department?

44) What are the most important problems to solve first?

45) What will be the greatest challenge in this job?

46) What would you expect me to accomplish in this job?

47) How often would we meet together?

48) What responsibilities have the highest priority?

49) How might these responsibilities and priorities change?

50) How much time should be devoted to each area of responsibility?

51) What are some examples of the achievements of others who have been in this position?

52) How many people have held this job in the last five years? Where are they now?

53) Why isn't this job being filled from within?

54) What are the traits and skills of people who are the most successful within the organisation?

55) Are there any difficult personalities on the staff?

56) How many employees would I supervise?

57) If this position is offered to me, why should I accept it?

58) What do you see in my personality, work history or skill set that attracts you to me?

59) How soon do you expect to make a decision?

60) If I am offered the position, how soon will you need my response?

Finally, you may want to discuss issues of compensation. The following are some suggestions for questions pertaining to salary and benefit packages (only if you are interviewing for a very senior position in the company):

1) What are the benefits and perks?

2) What is the salary range?

3) What is my earnings potential in one, three, five and ten years?

If you have done your research well, you can make the most of this chance to display your knowledge and enthusiasm. But don't overdo this, don't take over, and don't show off. Having weathered all that had gone before, you do not now want to bore the interviewer, or leave him with the impression that you are a smart ?

Dumb Questions to ask

1) Is it possible for me to get a small loan?

2) What is it that your company does?

3) Can I see the mess room?

4) What are your psychiatric benefits?

5) How many warnings do you get before you are fired?

6) Can you guarantee me that I will still have a job a year from now?

7) Would anyone notice if I came in late and left early?

8) What does this company consider a good absenteeism record?

9) The job description mentions weekend work. Is it compulsory?

10) How do you define successful performance in this position?

11) Is there special training you require, or suggest for someone holding this position?

12) How does this department's objectives contribute to the overall company goals?

13) How will the current economic trend impact this department?

14) Which problems facing the industry will affect the organisation?

15) Could you tell me how long you have worked here for this company, and a little bit about how you grew into your current position?

16) What projects or goals will bring success to the department or team?

17) What is your feeling about how I would fit into this organisation?

18) Can you tell me more about the position and the type of person you are seeking?

19) Tell me about an employee in your organisation who is considered to be an outstanding employee. What makes him special?

20) What would you consider to be exceptional performance from someone performing in this position in the first 90 days?

21) How does my background compare with others you have interviewed?

22) Why did you decide to join this organisation?

23) I feel my background and experience are a good fit for this position, and I am very interested. I am ready to consider your best offer!

That last one is not a question. BUT if you have not said it yet, you better say it at the end of the interview!

22) Why did you decide to join this organisation?

17

Farewell And Follow - Up

"The greatest thing in this world is not so much where we stand as in what direction we are moving." — *Oliver Wendall Holmes*

The closing phase is the most important part of the interview for making a lasting impression that can place you above other competitors for the same position. Let the interviewer know how excited you are about the position, and that you want the job. Then find out what the next step is.

Do try and get business cards from each person you interviewed with, or at least the correct spelling of their names.

Finally, as you are learning, tell them how much you would enjoy working with them personally. And don't forget to thank the receptionist or assistant on your way out. And to be a real hit, use their names if you know them. It always helps to be friends with these folks, since they are the ones who screen calls and messages.

After the interview, make notes right away so that you don't forget crucial details. Take stock of how you have done. Highlight what went well and what could have been improved on. Then think how you could cope more effectively, and use the experience positively for your next interview.

It is amazing how many job-seekers skip the crucial step

of a follow-up. You must immediately write a 'thank you' note to each person who interviewed you. Not only is this letter part of professional etiquette, but it is often time to reinforce a concept or skill that you have, and that the employer desires in the person they will be hiring. It is good to keep the letter short to also reiterate your interest in the position and your confidence in your qualifications. The simple gestures of a phone call and thank you letter can make a big difference in separating you from your competitors. After all, the employer took a chunk out of his day to give you a chance to win a job. So, this is the time for you to say 'thanks' in writing.

If the employer said that he would have a decision in a week, don't call him back immediately, but call him in a week, again to thank him (or them) for the interview, reiterating your interest.

If you receive word that another candidate was chosen, you may also send a follow-up letter to that employer, again thanking him for the opportunity to interview for the position. Let them know that should another or similar position open in the future, you would love to have the opportunity to interview again.

Once an offer of employment has been made, it is usually subject to satisfactory references, which are taken as a matter of course. The offer should include all the details required by law, together with a contract of employment. As the prospective employer, issue the candidate with two copies of the offer letter, one of which should be signed and returned to you by the candidate indicating his starting date.

Once you have received the signed letter, it is recommended that you send a post acceptance letter to the candidate welcoming him to your company, and providing details of when and where he should start work, and who he should report to on his first day.

Other Books on

QUIZ & CAREERS

Unit No. 220, Second Floor, 4735/22,
Prakash Deep Building, Ansari Road, Darya Ganj,
New Delhi - 110002, Ph.: 32903912, 23280047, 09811594448
E-mail: lotus_press@sify.com, www.lotuspress.co.in